mud in your eye!
prosit!
salud!
skaal!
pura quanzu!
a votre santé!
eviva!
nazdravica!
mabuhay!
proost!

Whatever the language, the meaning's the same —"Drink up!" Here's the complete comprehensive guide to good drinking.

Of the famous Esquire Drink Book, on which THE ART OF MIXING DRINKS is based, one reviewer said:

"Gay and sophisticated—a gem of a book! For the lady who wants to give a certain gentleman something he can treasure and use, I can think of no more fitting book. For gents who wish their friends would serve fewer and better drinks, this is a splendid book to give. If the reader thinks this is an unqualified approval—**it is!**"

—Philadelphia News

THE ART OF
MIXING DRINKS

BASED ON
ESQUIRE DRINK BOOK

THE ART OF MIXING DRINKS
(*based on* ESQUIRE DRINK BOOK)

A Bantam Book / published November 1957
2nd printing ..... January 1958
New Bantam edition published December 1960
2nd printing ... December 1960
3rd printing ... December 1961
Bantam Reference Library edition published December 1962
5th printing ... December 1962
6th printing ..... January 1964
7th printing ..... January 1965
8th printing .... February 1966
9th printing .... February 1967
Revised Bantam edition published October 1967
11th printing .... July 1968
12th printing .... July 1968
13th printing .. November 1968
14th printing .... October 1969
15th printing .... October 1970
16th printing ..... August 1971
17th printing ..... August 1971
18th printing ...... April 1972

Published simultaneously in the United States and Canada

Bantam Books are published by Bantam Books, Inc., a National General company. Its trade-mark, consisting of the words "Bantam Books" and the portrayal of a bantam, is registered in the United States Patent Office and in other countries. Marca Registrada. Bantam Books, Inc., 666 Fifth Avenue, New York, N.Y. 10019.

PRINTED IN THE UNITED STATES OF AMERICA

CONTENTS

THE ART OF MIXING DRINKS

THE MAGIC TOUCH

There are good drinks and bad drinks—sometimes of the very same ingredients, just as there are good and bad bars which serve the same drinks. So it is the host's obligation to create this difference for his guests, since we are assuming that his entertaining is of his own choosing, rather than the drinks wrenched from him by self-invited guests who have mistaken his home for the country club.

For the spongers, give them the worst you have, short of poisoning them. If they like your stuff too much, they might come back too often. Never mind your reputation as a bartender: it might suffer, but so will your bank account if these characters figure you out for a good thing. And use your smallest glasses; these louts are always fast talkers and fast drinkers, and the more ice water you give them, the better.

But now let us speak more sternly, in the matter of your own good friends. Nothing should be too good for them. Do not buy cheap stuff and put it in expensive bottles, or in glass decanters, no matter how beautiful, for your crime will be found out and your shame far greater than if you had the force of character—backed by the squeals from your budget—to put before them modestly priced stuff.

But do put out the good stuff, even if you must entertain less often. Display your bottles proudly and with nary a clinker among them. There is no more subtle or solid way of telling your friends how highly you regard them. If it's to be an all-night brawl for a mob, all right—give them anything and everything. But we're thinking most of a congenial gathering in your house, not a witches' dance on Bald Mountain.

Some hosts merely tell the boys to dip in and fix their own. This is not too bad for a summer evening when practically everyone is having a long tall one and one guy just hasn't got the energy to go sailing out and around every time the bottom of a dry glass heaves in view.

But we suggest that you mind your business of being the host —and *be* the host. Keep busy and keep them filled and keep them happy. Dear old Harry, who is always drunk at his own parties and won't let you go home when your eyeballs are turning to glue, may have a big heart and maybe even a big head in the morning, but may be pint-size as a host. Your turn to enjoy yourself will come: it's best to enjoy the art of being the best damn bartender in the county.

Now let us take the broad view on entertaining. You can curl up with a good bottle by yourself, and have a fair time reviewing past loves and future triumphs. But most of us are able to do this without undue planning or any stress and strain on the wardrobe, much less reference to a book of etiquette.

Let us be more expansive. Don Quixote said: "I drink upon occasion and sometimes I drink upon no occasion!" If you've just got the urge for a party, the last chapter in this volume will offer you 532 excuses for one: there is no excuse for not having one.

But there are times when you have a cocktail party thrust upon you: a sudden onslaught of family members, a delicate hint by your boss that he and the missus will be motoring in your vicinity and would appreciate some refreshment, a sudden light in the eye of a suddenly beautiful dame, and other spontaneous and sometimes spectacular challenges. For these, we give you *Esquire's* own *What & When Chart,* your advisor and friend in need. Even if you are not facing an emergency, it won't hurt to glance over this chart. You'll know then where the word is waiting for you, in case the blow falls.

Let's assume that you've sent out your invitations—printed, penned or phoned. (Engraving is impressive, but takes weeks.) Can be sizable card or folder, plain or decorated, bearing genial salutations. Or a practical but presentable "informal" (small and folded, titled with your name). States day, time (usually 4-6 or 5-7), and place, with mention of cocktails. And don't forget R.S.V.P. if you care. Invitations should be issued one to two weeks in advance.

Population Estimate: To be on the safe side, add 10 or 20 per cent to the number of acceptances. Or, if you're operating without R.S.V.P.'s, count on about 70 per cent of the crowd putting in an appearance. In any case, one sound theory says that the party should either be small enough so everyone can be seated or large enough so that the standees won't prove embarrassing.

Glassware: You need at least two to a customer of shapes and sizes required by the pouring program: 3-ounce cocktail stemmers (busiest), 10-ounce highball glasses (close competitors), 2-ounce V-glasses for sherry, Old Fashioned glasses (if you're serving that drink), champagne glasses if festivity is ultra.

Beverage Supplies: Three drinks per person is a fair allowance. You compute the bottles without calculus if you know your clue numbers. Basic 17 is the number of jiggers (1½ ounces each) that a "fifth" bottle (25.6 ounces) will pour. Translated, it means 17 Martinis per bottle of gin 17 Daiquiris per bottle of rum, 17 Manhattans or Old Fashioneds per bottle of whiskey. If brandy or Scotch highballs are of 1-jigger strength, 17 washes up the bottle.

But let's be larger-minded, tripling our jiggers to 51 and throwing away the spare, which would probably be accounted for by spillage anyhow. Now our yardstick is 50 drinks, 3 bottles—offering an easy jump to 200 drinks, 1 case. But the vermouths, dry for the Martinis and sweet for the Manhattans, are still to be reckoned. They operate at half-jigger speed: 34 cocktails (clue 17 doubled) to the "fifth," or 40 to the taller traditional "vermouth bottle" which is 2 ounces short of a quart; 50 cocktails therefore mean 1½ "fifths" of vermouth, or 1¼ traditional size, along with the 3 bottles of liquor; and the case job of 200 would require 6 vermouth "fifths" or 5 traditionals.

Sherry deals are 2-ounce, a dozen to the bottle, with a residue of 1.6 ounces, which in old Spanish sherries may be dreggy. American sherries run younger and can usually be squeezed to the last drop, providing a starter on the next glass; so count 25 for 2 bottles. Similarly 2 "fifths" of liquor will yield 25 highballs of 2-ounce strength. (More appropriate for a stag affair than a mixed party.) Champagne, straight or cocktailed, is 6-9 to the bottle.

At a big cocktail party, a choice of drinks should be available. It's a safe bet to offer:

1 *standard cocktail* (Martini, Manhattan, or Old Fashioned)
1 *other cocktail,* either standard or more fanciful
Whisky and soda, for the long drinkers
An apéritif, for the mild drinkers (sherry or Dubonnet)
A non-alcoholic drink for the wagon-riders

Fruit and Fixings: Maraschino cherries for Manhattans and Old Fashioneds; pitted olives for Martinis; 1 lime to 2 Daiquiris or 2 Cuba Libres: 2 sizable lemons to 3 Collinses; snips of lemon peel and half-slices of oranges for Old Fashioneds. Large bottle of bitters. Sugar. Bottles of sparkling water, prechilled.

Ice: More than you could expect of your refrigerator. If you live in a city, phone a cube service; in the country, your ice company will oblige. Shakers and mixing glasses require cracked ice.

Flowers: By all means, but vased where they won't be knocked over.

Cigarettes: Invitingly stood up in shot glasses in many strategic spots. Ash trays everywhere. Matches, table lighters.

Canapés: Liquor stimulates the hunger. Therefore, it is a gesture toward your guests to provide them with a snack. It is just precaution to furnish them with a little sustenance which will stay their heebie-jeebies. We deal with this in a separate chapter entitled "Aftermath," in which the defensive aspccts of a stomach with a bit of food in it are discussed.

But let's put it more simply. It makes your party better. More generous. More colorful. It keeps people moving about, and gives them a chance to escape the bores, and the bores to find new victims.

But let us also reflect. A box of crackers and some rat cheese, no matter how robustly you may proclaim this as your personal preference, is not going to remind your guests of a Lucullan banquet.

Let us reflect further. You can buy frozen hors d'oeuvres, which after a spell in the oven, taste like hot soap instead of cold soap. Or you can have that widder-woman from the other side of town prepare a few trays and you can modestly admit them to be your own. In this case, just don't wait around for questions as to the recipe, and by all means don't employ an unpunctual widder-woman who delivers her wares in the middle of your party and who stays on to ask the guests how they like her work. They might wind up in her house.

No. If you want to be simple about it, get a fine cheese as big as a wagon wheel, and put ten thousand crackers, and a dozen silver knives, around it; get a bucket of caviar, and surround it with slivers of lemon, shredded raw white onion to dust on it, more thousands of crackers, and butter knives. At least, with this you've admitted that you're lazy but that you're willing to spend some dough on your guests.

Warning: Do not make up chicken salad, tunafish salad, mixed-cream-cheese-olive-sawdust-combination salad, spread on bread, cut off the crust, and then slice into little oblongs or triangles. Your guests will hate you forever, and quite rightly.

Warning: After a number of drinks, people will not eat tidbits. After a point, if you wish them to stay, you must serve ham, roast turkey, chicken à la king, lobster Newburg, or dinner. Do not attempt to foist off on some gentleman who is standing aloof—visualizing a broiled sirloin—a bit of deviled egg, only slightly speckled with cigarette ashes.

In other words, do it right, or don't do it.

Confusion Control: If you live in an apartment house, you can save yourself a lot of running every time the bell rings, if you leave the front door open. The parking of coats and hats will be simplified if guests, as they enter, can see at a glance where they are to lay their things. Perhaps on tables (or borrowed hat racks) by the door—or placed right out in the hall—if you can trust your neighbors! If coats are to be put in bedrooms, have signs conspicuously displayed bearing arrows, one reading "Boys," the other "Girls." If your party is large and formal, then, of course, you will hire a checker. But if you indulge in such swank, then you're probably going to put yourself in the hands of professionals—caterers and such—and you won't need these helps.

Now here's the fourteen drinks you should be prepared to mix at some time in your career as host. Pretty basic stuff —much of this you'll know—but let's get them out where we can see them, anyway.

Cocktail: Before lunch or dinner, cocktails relax the spirit, whet the appetite. Generally made with one of the basic liquors in 1-to-5-to-1 proportions with vermouth, bitters, etc. Always chilled.

Cooler: As the name implies, it's a long, well-iced summer drink. Made with port, claret, sherry, sloe gin, or any of the basic liquors, ice, sugar, lemon, and club soda in 12- to 14-ounce glass.

Flip: For the most part, a lady's drink, but don't neglect it. Best made in an electric blender—a whole egg, sugar, cracked ice, and sherry, applejack, or whiskeys. Sour glass. Add spice.

Highball: One of the simplest drinks in your recipe book, but one of the most satisfying. Whiskeys, gin, brandy, or rum served with ice cubes or cracked ice and club soda, ginger ale, or cola.

Punch: The ideal beverage for parties—summer or winter. Usually made with fruit, chilled club soda, a block of ice, bitters, sugar, cherries, and brandy, wines, rum, or whiskeys. Mix carefully.

Sangaree: A quiet drink with a delayed action. Most sangarees are made with wine, sugar syrup, and ice in 8-ounce glass. Dust with nutmeg. Brandy and gin have been similarly well combined.

Sour: Something of a cocktail, too, but also a highly satisfactory drink at any time. Whiskeys, rum, applejack, brandy, or gin mixed with juice of half a lemon, ice, sugar, orange slice, and a cherry.

Collins: The summer soldier, very tall, very cold. Made with 3 or 4 ounces of rum, gin, whiskeys, brandy, or applejack, with sugar, lemon, or lime juice, chilled club soda in 12- or 14-ounce glass.

Fizz: This one bubbles, gives pleasure and relaxation in midafternoon or evening. Made with gin, rum, wines, or whiskeys, plus fruit syrups or sugar, ice, lime or lemon, club soda, egg white.

Frappé and *On-the-Rocks:* Popular drinks made by pouring any of your favorite alcoholic beverages over finely cracked ice in cocktail glass (frappé) or over ice cubes in an Old Fashioned glass (on-the-rocks).

Julep: Naturally, this one came out of Kentucky but it is cool and refreshing anywhere. Mix fresh mint with crushed ice and bourbon or rye in an 8-ounce glass. Garnish again with fresh mint.

Rickey: Another tall, cool treat for the summer months. Simple and delightful, the ricky requires the juice and rind of half a lime, ice cubes, and gin or whiskeys in a 6- or 8-ounce glass.

Sling: A sort of cocktail with gin, whiskeys, brandy, applejack, or rum poured over a dissolved lump of sugar, ice, lemon juice, water, and bitters, if desired. Make each in an Old Fashioned glass.

Toddy: With a quiet evening, toddies, hot or cold, are ideal. Dissolve lump sugar in little water in Old Fashioned glass, add ice or hot water, basic liquor, clove, nutmeg, cinnamon, lemon peel.

And now that we've taken a good look at all of them. here's how:

Order of procedure: In mixing drinks, put in the less costly ingredients first—thus if you make a mistake you can start again with a minimum of loss. Let's illustrate with a specific drink—say a Brandy Egg Nog. The recipe calls for:

> 1 jigger of cognac, 1 teaspoon of sugar, 5 ounces milk, 1 whole egg, cracked ice, nutmeg. First the ice goes in, then (2) milk, (3) sugar, (4) egg,—and last of all—the cognac. The nutmeg in this case is decoration, not an ingredient. Exceptions to this rule are drinks in which one ingredient is floated on top of another—as in the Pousse-Café.

Also, for the sake of chemistry, when mixing drinks containing fruit juices, and/or sweetening, *always* pour the spirits last.

Eggs: It takes practice to extract the white of an egg with grace and dispatch. Break the egg by hitting the center on the edge of a glass, splitting it into two equal parts, then pass the yoke from one half-shell to the other until the white seeps through to a container below. The egg always goes into a mixing glass before the liquor. If bad there is time to throw it away before expensive spirits have converted an accident into a financial loss—or what is worse, a social catastrophe.

How to Float Brandy or Liqueur: To make brandy float on crème de menthe or other liqueurs, tilt glass slightly, insert a teaspoon bottom-side up, and pour brandy slowly over the rounded surface. To make a Pousse-Café of six colors put 1/6 ounce grenadine at bottom of Pousse-Café glass, insert glass stirring rod, and carefully pour over it the following ingredients in order: 1/6 ounce of crème de cacao, ditto maraschino, menthe, crème Yvette. Top with cognac.

Rub the top edge of bottles with waxed paper when you open them, since this prevents dripping. To further avoid spillage, twist the bottle to right or left as you complete pouring. When opening soda, tilt the bottle to conserve the sparkle,

Always use salt and water in washing beer glasses; soap tends to flatten beer. Also, it is wise to wet the glass before pouring the beer to prevent it from going flat.

To open a rare old bottle of wine without disturbing the sediment, or to remove a stubborn cork, grip the neck of the bottle under the flange for about half a minute with bottle tongs flame-heated to the glowing point. Then apply a cold wet cloth to the bottle neck. The top of the bottle will snap off cleanly.

Never fill a half-empty wine glass. Mixing cold wine with warm detracts from the full enjoyment of the wine. It is not wise to decant two bottles of wine into the same decanter since a bottle of wine may thus lose its individual character. Buckshot should be used in cleaning a decanter, never soda or soap.

Measuring: One jigger—1½ ounces
Pony—1 ounce
Teaspoon—⅛ ounce
Dash—⅙ teaspoon

With practice you can learn to measure accurately by the movement of your arm. If, when shaking, you find yourself short on quantity, shake longer—thus stretching the drink by melting more ice.

Stirring: Any drink or cocktail whose ingredients are clear liquors requires only stirring with ice for proper mixing. The Stinger is one of the few exceptions to this rule. Drinks to be shaken are those containing fruit, eggs, cream, or any other ingredients difficult to blend.

Pouring: There is no protocol for pouring a drink into a glass. However, when mixing a batch for four or more, it is necessary to have mixture of same consistency in each glass. To assure this, set all glasses in a row on bar, edges touching. Pour each drink halfway, then go back to the first and level off. Poured this way, all drinks are even-bodied—you don't get just the top layer in the first glass and heavier liquid in the others.

Shaking: The best type of shaker to use is a bartender's shaker. This consists of two containers; the ingredients go into one, the ice into the other. Cocktails that require shaking should be shaken well so that they come out creamy. Wash ice before using; then shake to eliminate excess water. Water can ruin a drink.

Ice: Use shaved ice for drinks that are to be sipped through a straw; cubed ice for highballs and the Old Fashioned; cracked ice for the in-betweens. If you use a bar shaker, put the ice in one container, the ingredients to be mixed in the other—then bring the two together and shake. Be sure that the ice is fresh and well washed. Ice cubes left too long in the freezing compartment of a refrigerator tend to acquire a peculiar "icebox flavor." Whenever possible, use fresh cubes.

To Chill a Glass: All cocktail glasses should be well chilled. Before mixing a cocktail, fill each glass with shaved ice. Let the glass stand while the drink is being prepared. When the mixture is ready, empty the glass, wipe it carefully—then pour. Properly chilled glasses make all drinks more appetizing.

The Frosted Glass: Glasses for "frosted" drinks should be stored in the refrigerator or buried in the shaved ice. For "sugar-frosted" glass, dampen rim of the precooled glass with slice of lemon. Dip glass into a bowl of powdered sugar, leave for a second, and thump to get rid of excess.

The Strainer: All cocktails should be strained before serving. Use a wire strainer—not silver. The ideal strainer for home use is one with clips which allow the wire to extend over the edge of the glass. The strainer is held over the shaker. One finger on top holds it steady. Handle is between the fingers.

Sugar: Sugar always goes into the shaker before the liquor. Powdered sugar should be used—unless the recipe states otherwise. Simple syrup is not recommended, except where specified. Powdered sugar blends quickly and has a better effect in the cocktail. Keep simple syrup around, though—just in case.

When making Old Fashioneds, place the setups to be served in the drink in the refrigerator for an hour or so before serving. When ready to serve, just add the whiskey. The drink will be better because the glasses and fruit are thoroughly chilled.

For a really frosted mint julep, prepare ingredients in glass with cracked ice. Set glass in shaved ice and stir until glass frosts.

The Egg and You: In shaking a drink which requires an egg, use a whole cube of ice to break up and blend the egg with the other ingredients. You might also try the following egg trick on drinking companions: Place in a sherry glass one hard-boiled egg, on the upper end of which you have pencil-marked an X. Challenge your nearest neighbor to invert the egg, so that the X is on the bottom, without touching egg or glass or pouring liquid into the glass. When neighbor belligerently claims it can't be done, put your money on the table. While standing up, lean over the glass, and blow once very hard directly down on top of the egg. Since the egg and glass don't make a perfect fit, air pressure is built up below the egg when you blow on it, and flips the egg over. Collect your cash, and give the egg to the loser.

On-the-House Cocktail: Take the usual bartender's cocktail shaker, composed of a glass container and metal cap. In the metal cap, while unobserved, stuff a bar towel. Then, with many a flourish, mix a drink in the glass using coloring matter, ice and water, so that no valuable spirits will be wasted; make certain the audience follows every move. Now place the metal half of the shaker on top of the glass container, and shake vigorously. Remove glass container, place strainer on metal shaker and pour. Nothing, but nothing, comes out—the secret being, of course, that the bar towel has absorbed the "drinks."

And for your final calculations, and to settle divers arguments, here are the basic measures:

1 quart	32 ounces
1/5	25.6 ounces
1 pint	16 ounces
1 pony	1 ounce
1 jigger	1½ ounces
1 wineglass	4 ounces
1 teaspoonful	1/8 ounce
1 dash	1/6 teaspoonful

Standard Sizes of Glasses

Whiskey	1 oz. to 2½ oz.
Cocktail	2 oz. to 3½ oz.
Sherry	2 oz. to 2½ oz.
Champagne	5 oz. to 6 oz.
Cordial	¾ oz. to 1 oz.
Delmonico	5 oz. to 7 oz.
Old Fashioned	4 oz. to 6 oz.
Highball	8 oz. to 10 oz.

Tom Collins	10 oz. to 14 oz.
Goblet	8 oz. to 12 oz.
Tumbler	8 oz. to 12 oz.
Sauterne	4 oz.
Claret	4 oz.
Pony	1 oz.

WHAT AND WHEN

GLAD-HANDERS, CLOSE FRIENDS AND NEIGHBORS

Cocktail Hour: Usual guest preferences, but you might suggest Jack Rose or Sazarac cocktails. Serve Smorgasnacks. South African Veldt music is excellent for listening or for background.

Sunday Brunch: Go light on liquor with Sherry Flip or Milk Punch. Accent on food. Whip up orange pancakes, eggs on the side or French-fried sandwiches served with sausages. Serve in sunlight if possible.

After Sports: Dubonnet or Whiskey Sour for relaxing. Strong appetites can handle a man-sized hors d'oeuvre like hamburger balls on toothpicks. If it's winter, a hot Tom and Jerry, with a log on the fire.

Midweek Evening: Liven up the bridge game with Madeira and Bacardis. Chicken-feed sandwiches: diced chicken, chopped peanuts, penny-sized slices of black olives, and mayonnaise. And try conversation!

Midsummer Siesta: Greet returning swimmers or awakening lollers with a heart-lifting Planter's Punch or Singapore Sling. Sandwiches and snowballs (shaved ice packed into balls and drenched with liqueurs) are a bell-ringing combination.

After the Theatre: Hook up the home recorder and let each give his version of the star of the evening. Porter or stout with a midnight snack will bring down the curtain.

The Outdoor Grill: Let them try their luck at archery or target shooting. Reward high scorers with small broiled fish, butter or sauce basted, and applejack. Don't forget the portable radio.

The Stirrup Cup: Hair of the dog (one more of the same). A Sherry Flip, or a bracer of stout or ale are restful parting shots.

FAMILY, ELDERS, IN-LAWS, COUNTRY COUSINS

Cocktail Hour: Pink Lady, dry sherry or Dubonnet for the ladies; Bourbon Toddy for the men. Harlequin Eggs (hard-boiled eggs stuffed with grated carrots, beans, beets mixed with mayonnaise) will excite pleased murmurs.

Sunday Brunch: Sherry Eggnog goes nicely here. Suggest French Toast with honey or cinnamon and sugar. Cut flowers for the table.

After Sports: Round out your family circle with Mulled Claret or Sloe Gin Fizzes. For a winner, put crisp bacon and thin tomato slabs between slices of hazelnut toast.

Midweek Evening: Only to the family are home movies a treat, so don't miss the chance while they're sipping Dubonnet frappé or Travel wine. Might do some home recording, too, for a future playback.

Midsummer Siesta: Try that snowball trick (above) on the elders, using very sweet wine for the ladies. The Sherry Flip goes well, too, with a tray of light canapés. Turn on easy but thoughtful music—Manhattan Towers for instance.

After the Theatre: Plant a platter of cold fried chicken and potato salad in the ice-box, and casually suggest a "raid-the-ice-box" party. Sherry Flip or Madeira for sipping while they reminisce on the stars of yesteryear.

The Outdoor Grill: Give them a choice of Presidente cocktail, ginger beer, or Riesling wine while they watch you spit-turn a chicken with chestnut dressing. A cool bottle of white wine goes well.

The Stirrup Cup: An egg drink is always good here. Try a Port Flip or a Brandy Milk Punch.

BUSINESS, VISITING FIREMEN, PROSPECTS, TYCOONS

Cocktail Hour: Champagne cocktails or Daiquiris fit in well here. Let the talk take its course against a background of recorded Debussy. The ladies will each remember a single gardenia from a corsage bowl centerpiece.

Sunday Brunch: Black Velvet (half-and-half stout and champagne) will impress; a White Lady will soothe. Try a fine omelet, with a side order of fried ham topped with fried pineapple and bananas.

After Sports: As they recall the plays, serve Sazaracs or Bourbon Toddies with silver souvenir spoons that become keepsakes for your guests. Hot canapés.

Midweek Evening: Invite them in for a good fight or an exciting game on the television set; for a special symphony or musical evening on the records. A Brandy and Soda or a Black Velvet slip in nicely here.

Midsummer Siesta: Undisputed aristocrat of any midsummer siesta is the immortal Mint Julep. Nothing need go with it, and nothing much can follow it. If your mint bed's especially fine, pack a few roots for the guests to take home.

After the Theatre: Crayfish bisque (canned) will rate top reviews for you. Follow through with a French 75, Fine Champagne Cognac. Dancing and demitasse may wind up the evening.

The Outdoor Grill: Vermouth Cassis or a specially fine dry sherry are excellent outdoor appetizers for French-fried shrimp or roasted game bird. Turn the yard into a picnic ground complete with colorful table under the trees.

The Stirrup Cup: For a lasting last impression—Crusted Port!

ROYALTY, POTENTATES, HIGH SOCIETY

Cocktail Hour: For that once-in-a-lifetime occasion, splurge with champagne, or a Crème de Menthe Frappé with a V.O. Brandy Float. If high royalty and the setting permits, import two or three musicians, and hand-pick the program.

Sunday Brunch: Champagne—no less. A caviar omelet is fit for a king, with brandied fruit, coffee and whipped cream. A copy of the morning paper for each, and symphonic music. Don't forget the flowers.

After Sports: Cognac VVO and Golden Fizz after the game will get a royal reception—as will patty shells filled with diced duck, almonds, and mayonnaise, topped with capers and water cress.

Midweek Evening: Don't stand on ceremony; come out boldly with a French 75 and B & B. Or make the party really memorable with a flaming Café Brûlé (described on another page). Here's a chance to start a guest book with a star lead-off.

Midsummer Siesta: After they've watched you play the local flash at tennis, or heard the Boston Pops play Brahms, they will welcome rum-soaked pineapple balls. In the drink department: Mint Julep again! In thickly frosted silver glasses.

After the Theatre: Quietly produce a chilled bottle of vintage Sparkling Burgundy, Armagnac. A neat idea is melon balls in the same white Burgundy. Some background Mozart, and you might give thought to a toast for your special guests.

The Outdoor Grill: Show what your grill can do with smoked turkey, game fowl or venison. And in the hand, imported Quinine Water or Wine Cooler (crushed fruit and wine). Some hired music would do well here, if the occasion is especially special.

The Stirrup Cup: A split of champagne, by all means! And a bit of fine glass as a gift for each of your regal friends will be long remembered—especially if they've already admired it, and you've wrapped it without their knowing it.

ALL STAG

Cocktail Hour: In a roomful of Men of Distinction, switch to Frisco, New Yorker or Sazarac, with highballs on the side. Stock up with stories and serve the Boston sandwich: ham, turkey and Swiss cheese on rye.

Sunday Brunch: For an eye opener, stag brunchers may want a prairie oyster, an eggnog, or tomato juice spiked with Worcestershire. Poached eggs are safe. And a quiet game of croquet, a swim or a walk will get circulation up.

After Sports: Wafer-thin strips of French-fried pork fat are better than potato chips. Especially with an Applejack Old Fashioned or Ward Eight. A few rounds of the horse-racing game or backgammon will lower sporting blood pressure.

Midweek Evening: Decorate the poker table with Beer-and-a-Bite. For blue-chip players keep Canadian whiskey or Bourbon 'n Bitters handy. Gershwin is good.

Midsummer Siesta: Cheeseburgers will take the edge off appetites whetted by spirited horseshoe pitching or hammock swinging. A Rickey will go well here; or a Planter's Punch.

After the Theatre: Cold roast (lamb, beef, turkey) sandwiches, with some hearty slugs of Irish whiskey and ale. And try them at composing a limerick, if the evening sags.

The Outdoor Grill: Set up a target range with nonlethal pistols and guns. Let them compete for choice cuts of genuine old-time two-inch-thick beefsteak with good red *vin ordinaire.* Top off with brandy in coffee.

The Stirrup Cup: "On the Rocks" for the stags, or a Whiskey Mist. Whatever it is, make it in base the same that they've had before. Coffee and brandy if the evening has been long and there's driving to be done.

ROMANCE

Cocktail Hour: She'll see things your way after Champagne cocktails. Let her grow strong on chicken-stuffed tomatoes, then weaken her with Strauss waltzes. Don't forget the corsage.

Sunday Brunch: Pink Lady will put the lady in the pink—or a split of champagne for two. Turn on some light, gay music, fill the bowl with flowers and the lady with an omelet soufflé.

After Sports: Dancing is an easy transition; slow music. Suggest a Sherry Flip; or, if thirsty, Cuba Libres under the umbrella. No politics or heavy conversation. Remember, she's tired.

Midweek Evening: Crème de Menthe Frappé with a brandy float, or a Spritzer (Rhine wine and soda). Take the pocket radio with you for a walk, or go prowling in out-of-the-way bypaths. Whatever you do, *make it memorable.*

Midsummer Siesta: Halved apricots poached in syrup and steeped in Cognac will fix her wagon in the middle of the afternoon. Consider also a Sloe Gin Fizz or a Spritzer, or—if you love the girl—that same Mint Julep!

After the Theatre: The show's over; now it's time for *your* play. As a curtain raiser, boldly enter with a Zombie. Second act, scrambled eggs with deviled ham. You'll have to write Act III yourself, but a Pousse Café might open it.

The Outdoor Grill: Partridge or pheasant for your favorite quail. If you're picnicking, take along a thermos of chilled vintage wine with two Bohemian glasses. She'll keep hers as a souvenir of the occasion. If she loses it, that's memorable too.

The Stirrup Cup: And one for the road! Where shall it lead and what shall it be? Sherry? Aspirin and water? An Angel's Kiss? Turn to the 1001 Recipes for Drinks from A to Z, close your eyes, flip a page or two, and pick a drink recipe at random. Then multiply by 10—and what can *you* lose?

BAR EXAMINATION

Even before you begin to pour, you need an arsenal of weapons to make the downing of your drinks downier.

Of course, you have a number of them on hand right now. But there are new ones coming out every day, so we've shopped about a bit and tried to bring you up to date on what's what on the whatnot.

Below are the standard outlines of your glass cabinet.

Of course, there are innumerable variations on this in style, quality, shape, and transparency. But we'd like to emphasize that—whatever your taste; modern, traditional, or eccentric —you have on hand a selection of good glassware. It just isn't true that good drinks taste just as good in ordinary glassware. Just as you will want to serve good basic liquors to your friends, so you will want to serve your drinks in containers worthy of your guests.

Glassware is not simply a matter of the manufacturer trying to steal your dough. The cocktail glass, for example, has a long stem so that the warmth of your hand will not detract from the delicious chill of the drink. Glass itself, being a very poor conductor of heat, is the perfect vessel for cold drinks as well as amplifying their visual effect by perfect clarity and subtle side-lighting. The solid Old Fashioned glass is perfectly designed for its rugged load of fruit and whiskey; the petite liqueur glass is the perfect expression of the liquid it bears.

Having got our back up on this subject of glassware, we're prepared to relax and say that if you're throwing a brawl, or particularly if you're having your party outdoors, it's just as well to have some run-of-the-mill glasses for breaking or dumping purposes. No need to sacrifice your choice crystal to the whims of a passel of satyrs chasing nymphs through the greenwood or standing on a table ready to be knocked aside by the tail-wagging of your neighbor's lovable but lunky Great Dane. Let 'em have Mr. Woolworth's best, in that case. But when you have your party under control, bring out your Tiffany or your Jensen or your Steuben or your Baccarat. Good glass is beautiful and not terribly expensive.

There's even a finer subdivision in buying glass. A man may enjoy a fine double Scotch Old Fashioned when he comes home after work, a big job full of ice—one for him, one for his wife—to restore sweetness to the soul and themselves to each other. Or maybe it can be a joy come some summer day to mix up a walloping Planter's Punch—San Juan style—in a sixteen-ounce glass, ready for a session on the greensward, when the mind swings south to the Caribbean and the thought of blue waters and islands springing from a sparkling sea.

But save these efforts for yourself. Don't serve *any* guest four-ounce Old Fashioneds or five-ounce tall drinks—or you'll have the house full of drunks in no time. They'll blame you, too. We remember a character who downed one after the other, spent the dinner hour behind a hedge, and his wife phoned the next day and accused us of serving him poisoned liquor.

So take it easy. Keep the drinks coming, normal size. And when it's time to turn to dinner, or to close up the house (you need a shave before you catch the 8:14 A.M.) use your enormous charm, and persuasion, and muscle—if necessary—to move your beloved guests toward the roast or their own roost. There's nothing worse than to stay up politely with a loquacious guest who jaws your head off and tells you every one of his well-worn jokes until all hours in the morning, and then the next time he sees you he laughs like hell and says he didn't remember a thing, funny, huh? haha! If *he* doesn't remember a thing, get him out of there and *you'll* be able to remember that you had a bit of sleep.

So let's spread out before us some of the glasses you may want to consider for your cabinet, and some of the beautiful gadgets that'll make serving a drink as pleasurable as driving out a hole in one. *Observez,* and compare the pictures with the captions. Almost every good bar accessory shop will have these primary tools, sandwiched in between nutcrackers shaped like you-know-what and aprons with funny sayings on them. This junk you can have if you want it: us, we suggest that you be yourself and concentrate on the drinks. They go down easier than corny cracks and horny gadgets that any clown with the price can buy.

Here's the stuff that looks right to us:

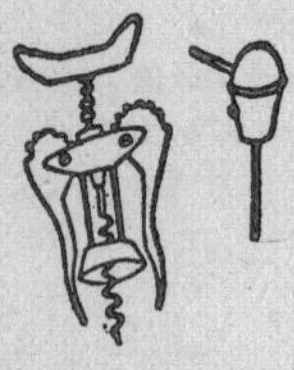

1. The art of drinking begins, logically enough, with opening the bottle. Hence the deluxe corkscrew. The automatic pourer measures a jigger—and only a jigger—at a time.

2. Three basic essentials for a well-equipped home bar are: a lime squeezer, a mixing spoon, and a double-ended measuring cup, for a jigger or a pony as required.

3. Preferred equipment, too, is a professional bar shaker with accompanying wire strainer. The Martini mixer is recommended for drinks that require stirring.

4. The cutting board should always be close at hand for ready preparation of fruit for drinks, for hors d'oeuvres, etc. It's also convenient to keep a disposal bin near by.

5. And when you're ready for the ice, adjust the icer for fine, medium or coarse, whatever the recipe calls for. Use it also for crushed ice for chilling glasses.

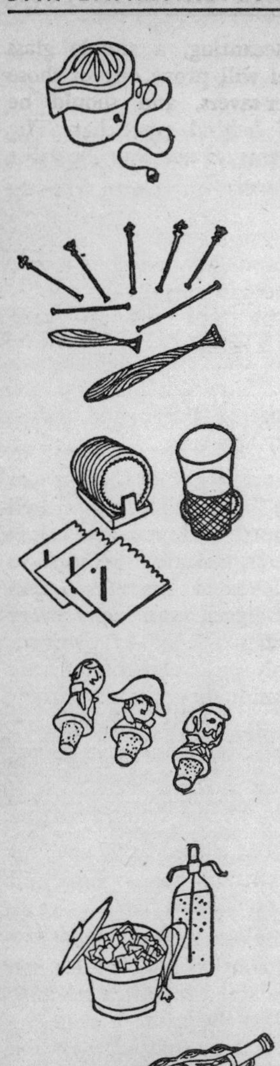

6. Always use fresh fruit juices in the drinks you make, never canned. This electric squeezer operates on AC-DC and is neat, clean and fast. It's a valuable bar aid.

7. Bar muddlers are made of lignum vitae, which is the hardest known wood. They are used in muddling sugar or in crushing mint. Glass ones are used as drink stirrers.

8. Masculine leather coasters are made of cowhide with saddle stitching and are water repellent. Jackets for the long drinks and napkins should not be forgotten.

9. And when the drinks have been made, the bottles can be recorked with decorative stoppers to dress up the bar. These stoppers are hand painted and colorful.

10. Without an ice bucket, confusion would reign. Also don't forget to have a supply of sparkling water on hand, either bottled or in the refillable syphon form.

11. A nice accessory touch for the serving of vintage wines is a wine cradle for use at the table. Wine can be poured without removing bottle from basket.

12. For decanting, a simple glass funnel will prove one of those temper-savers, and should be found behind every bar. The label around decanter identifies the contents.

13. And, as a last luxurious touch, the electric blender—the whiz kid, which can really give your drinks a whirl.

Now, maybe you'd like to step out a bit—set up a bar in your home without exactly going out and paying the price of a small car for one. So try this:

Built for rooms where space is precious, Esky's convertible corner bar is a compact, mobile item that ought to go high on your list of make-it-yourself projects. The bar (in black panel on next page) is easily made from material available in every town. Framing is simple lumber, sides are 1/4" fir plywood, top is 3/4" mahogany plywood, Novoply, or fir plywood, painted or stained. Sides are covered with flexible sheet plastic in color of your choice. Corner pieces (1/2" x 4" pine or birch) are blond mahogany—like the bar top. Adjust height of bar to your own comfort. The top has a wood well for ice and soda. Deep square cake pan (10" square) is used for ice, while an ordinary tin bread pan (7" x 10") holds bottles. Keep ice covered. The refrigerator is an electric automatic. Your exact inside dimensions will depend on which refrigerator you select. Note also the wire basket for soiled glasses, swivel sugar bowl secured to the underside of the bar top by a screw and washer, and the glass and gadget racks—all items available at hardware or dime stores. Bar doors are wood shutters, stained to match bar top. One door (whichever you choose) can be made a swinging door by putting dowels in the top and bottom edges of the door and set in holes in the top and bottom bar frame. This permits the door to swing 270 degrees if necessary. When both doors are closed, the bar converts to a buffet or sideboard, rolled around flat against one wall. These (both front and back views) features are also illustrated.

Here are four alternatives:

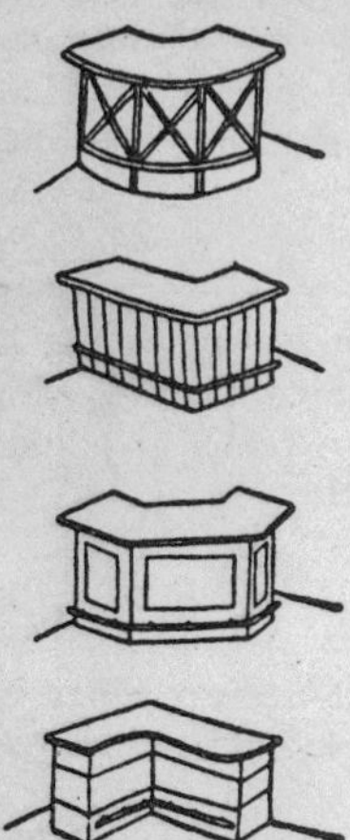

1. A drum bar, circular in shape with crisscross moldings of split bamboo.

2. An L-shaped bar, for larger parties, of random width, knotty pine boards.

3. A classic shape, which is easy to build and has no "unsocial" corners.

4. An inside L-shaped bar is most economical in terms of space: one long side faces the wall.

Now, sir, take your choice!

If you are heading for gracious living in a decisive way, we'd like to suggest that you keep wine in mind. Liquor is quicker, as Dorothy Parker says; but wine her is finer. And there's nothing like a cellar to give you that baronial air as you inspect the premises. And you can do it quite inexpensively, too. This way, sir:

1. *Cellar in a closet:* Cache your wine in the top half of any handy closet; stow a cordial cart below it. On the door hang a combination light and display for an especially noteworthy empty (the one that marked your first anniversary, perhaps), a shelf, and a tiltout bin for corkscrew and tools for opening cases.
2. *Vats in the basement:* Build a brace of truncated tuns for wine-keeping. Put them in the basement, the playroom, or the den. Notched boards or square cubbyholes hold corked bottles flat (so that the corks will be kept wet). The shelves contain jugs and screw tops. Post a wine inventory on the back of one door.
3. *New wine in old chests:* Launch an old radio cabinet or sideboard as a wine cellar. Add a flip-down workshelf

front, and prefabricated metal honeycomb racks. A small nook will hold worth-keeping wine lists from ships and your favorite restaurants. Upright bottles, a champagne cooler, and trays can be stored below.

DRINKS OF FAMOUS PEOPLE

BOB HOPE'S RYE LEMONADE

1 jigger rye. Mix with fresh lemonade. Add ice. Pour into glass whose rim was rubbed with lemon and sprinkled with sugar and left in refrigerator for at least a half-hour.

GARRY MOORE'S SCOTCH MILK PUNCH

Shake thoroughly 2 ounces Scotch and 6 ounces milk with sugar and ice. Pour into highball glass, and sprinkle drink with nutmeg.

JUDY HOLLIDAY'S WHITE LADY

3 to 4 parts gin with 1 part Cointreau and 1 part fresh grapefruit juice. Pour the mixture into a Martini glass.

BOB CROSBY'S KAILUA COCKTAIL

One and a half jiggers Puerto Rican dark rum, one jigger pineapple juice, 1/3 jigger lemon juice, 1/3 jigger of grenadine. Serve in punch cups.

RISE STEVENS' MORNING GLORY

Fill Collins glass with ice chunks, pour 1/2 ounce Cointreau, 1/2 ounce cherry brandy, dash of Angostura bitters. Add orange, pineapple slices. Fill with champagne.

BENNY GOODMAN'S ADMIRAL COCKTAIL

1 part bourbon, 2 parts dry vermouth, and juice of ½ lemon. Shake well with ice cubes. Pour. Lemon twist.

ART LINKLETTER'S PAPAYA COCKTAIL

Two parts of papaya juice, one part sherry wine. Serve in cocktail glass.

LILY PONS' CHAMPAGNE FRUIT PUNCH

Marinate 12 hours in ice box 2 quarts Chablis, 2 diced pineapples. Pour into bowl. Add quart Chablis, simple syrup, lemon juice to taste, dash cognac, two bottles of champagne.

KIM HUNTER'S RAINBOW OLD-FASHIONED

Pour over two ice cubes, 5 teaspoonfuls of water saturated with sugar (known as simple syrup).

Add 2 dashes Angostura bitters, 1 teaspoon maraschino cherry juice, 1 maraschino cherry, 2 ounces rye, half a slice of orange, a twist of lemon peel, and half a fresh strawberry. Stir twice gently and serve.

MANUEL KOMROFF'S CORONET COCKTAIL

2 parts gin, 1 part port wine. Stir with ice and peel of lemon. Do not shake.

SINCLAIR LEWIS' ARROWSMITH PUNCH

One-third pint lime or lemon juice, ¾ pound of sugar dissolved in water, half a pint of cognac, ¼ quart peach brandy, ¼ pint Jamaica rum, 2½ pints carbonated water. Add large piece of ice and serve from punch bowl.

MORLEY CALLAGHAN'S THEY SHALL INHERIT THE EARTH COCKTAIL

2 parts brandy, 2 parts lemon juice, 1 part Cointreau, 1 part Benedictine.

ALEXANDER WOOLLCOTT'S WHILE ROME BURNS COCKTAIL

1 part lemon juice, 2 parts Medford rum, 1 dash of maple syrup.

WILLIAM SEABROOK'S ASYLUM COCKTAIL

1 part gin, 1 part Pernod, dash of grenadine; pour over large lumps of ice. Do not shake.

DOUGLAS EDWARDS' ZOOMAR COCKTAIL

Shake jigger dark Puerto Rican rum, jigger pineapple juice, dash grenadine, dash lime, shaved ice. Serve in chilled glass.

GYPSY ROSE LEE'S VAN VLEET COCKTAIL

3 jiggers light rum, 1 jigger maple syrup, 1 jigger lemon juice. Shake well with cracked ice and serve like a Daiquiri. Prechill glass.

BURL IVES' LALLAH ROOKH COCKTAIL

In a shaker, chill a jigger of cognac with ½ jigger dark Barbados rum, teaspoon thick cream, ½ teaspoon sugar, pony of vanilla extract. Strain into cocktail glass with hollow stem.

PATRICE MUNSEL'S PLANTER'S PUNCH

1 part lime juice, 1 part brown sugar, 3 parts dark Jamaica rum, 3 parts of water. Stir sugar, water in pitcher. Add juice, ice and rum. Stir. Serve in tumblers or cocktail glasses.

ERNEST HEMINGWAY'S DEATH IN THE AFTERNOON COCKTAIL

Pour 1 jigger of absinthe into a champagne glass. Add iced champagne until it attains the proper opalescent milkiness. Drink 3 to 5 of these slowly.

ERSKINE CALDWELL'S TOBACCO ROAD COCKTAIL

Please observe closely the following procedure:

1. Select in May six of your finest McIntosh trees and place

a hive of bees under each tree to insure the setting of the blossoms.

2. Visit your trees with a spray gun once a month until October, and see to it that not an insect remains alive.

3. About the middle of October gather by hand four bushels of the finest "reds," selecting each apple for color, size, and ripeness.

4. When these are ready to put into the hopper of your cider mill, go back to the orchard and pick up two pecks of windfalls from the ground, carefully selecting the most decayed, wormiest, and snailencrusted.

5. Mix the two gatherings and grind and press.

6. For three days and nights drink the sweetest cider you have ever tasted, noting that no matter how much you drink, you can always find room for a little more.

7. On the fourth day you will discover that you have the hardest drink that ever blew a bung hole.

LOUIS PAUL'S PUMPKIN COACH COCKTAIL

2 parts liqueur Cesoriac, 1 part Italian vermouth, 1 part cherry juice, 3 limes (to each pint). Slathers of ice (or you will go home in a basket).

FRANK SCULLY'S FUN IN BED COCKTAIL

1 part grape juice, 1 part applejack. Ice, shake and serve.

OLIVER LA FARGE'S LAUGHING BOY COCKTAIL

Dissolve half a teaspoonful of sugar in a dash of Angostura bitters. Add 1 teaspoonful of sweet vermouth. Add chipped ice. Fill Old Fashioned glass to the brim with New England rum. Garnish with lemon peel and slices of orange (if you like fruit salad).

GUY LOMBARDO'S SOUPED-UP GIBSON

1 part vermouth, 4 parts gin, 6 pearl onions.

CARL CARMER'S
STARS FELL ON ALABAMA COCKTAIL

1 jigger old Alabama corn whiskey, 1 dash Peychaud bitters, 1 dash Angostura bitters, 1 dash orange flower water, 1 lump sugar, 6 drops absinthe. Ice and stir briskly.

NANCY BERG'S
VODKA ICEBERG

1 jigger vodka on rocks, dash of Pernod.

JANE PICKENS'
PICKENS' PUNCH

⅓ peach brandy, ⅓ cherry liqueur, ⅓ crème de menthe. Shake, then let stand for five minutes. Serve without ice.

1001 RECIPES FOR DRINKS FROM A TO Z

APPLEJACK

A. J.

½ applejack
½ unsweetened grapefruit juice
Grenadine to taste

Shake well with ice and strain into glass.

ANTE

½ Calvados or apple brandy
¼ Cointreau
¼ Dubonnet
1 dash Angostura bitters

Stir well with ice and strain into glass.

APPLE

⅓ Calvados or apple brandy
⅙ brandy
⅙ gin
⅓ sweet cider

Stir well with ice and strain into glass.

APPLE BLOW

2 jiggers applejack
4 dashes lemon juice
1 teaspoon sugar
1 egg white

Shake well with ice and strain into glass. Fill with soda water.

APPLE BRANDY COCKTAIL

4 parts apple brandy
1 part grenadine
1 part juice of lemon or lime

Agitate coolly and sieve.

APPLEJACK ALGONQUIN

1 teaspoon baked apple
1 lump sugar
1 jigger applejack

Fill glass with hot water. Sprinkle with nutmeg.

APPLEJACK COOLER

1 tablespoon sugar
Juice of ½ lemon
1 or 2 jiggers applejack

Shake well with cracked ice and strain into highball glass. Add ice cubes and fill with chilled soda water.

APPLEJACK DAISY

Juice ½ lemon
½ teaspoon powdered sugar
1 teaspoon grenadine
1 ounce applejack
1 ounce dry gin

Shake well with cracked ice and strain. Serve over ice cube, decorate with fruit.

APPLEJACK FLIP (FOR 2)

2⅔ jiggers applejack
1 egg
2 teaspoons sugar
½ cup shaved ice

Chill all ingredients and place in chilled container of electric blender. Cover and blend for 20 seconds. Pour into 6-ounce glasses and sprinkle with nutmeg.

APPLEJACK RABBIT

1 jigger applejack or apple brandy
⅓ jigger lemon juice
⅓ jigger orange juice
Maple syrup to taste

Shake well with ice and strain into glass.

APPLEJACK SOUR

2 jiggers applejack
Juice of ½ lime
Juice of ½ lemon
1 dash grenadine
½ teaspoon sugar

Shake well with ice and strain into Delmonico glass. Decorate with fruit if desired.

APPLE SWIZZLE

6 dashes Angostura bitters
1½ ounces apple brandy
1 ounce rum
Juice ½ lime
1 teaspoonful fine granulated sugar

Pour ingredients into a glass pitcher, add plenty of shaved ice, churn vigorously with a swizzle stick until the pitcher frosts. Strain into cocktail glass.

BARTON SPECIAL

½ Calvados or apple brandy
¼ Scotch whisky
¼ dry gin

Shake well with ice and strain into glass. Serve with twist of lemon peel.

BENTLEY

½ Calvados or apple brandy
½ Dubonnet

Stir well with ice and strain into glass.

CASTLE DIP

½ apple brandy
½ white crème de menthe
3 dashes Pernod

Shake well with ice and strain into glass.

COFFEE COCKTAIL

½ jigger apple brandy
½ jigger port wine
1 egg yolk

Shake well with cracked ice. Strain into cocktail glass. Flurry of nutmeg on top.

CORONATION

⅓ Italian vermouth
⅓ French vermouth
⅓ applejack
Dash of apricot brandy

DEAUVILLE

1 ounce apple brandy
1 teaspoon lemon juice
½ ounce Cointreau

Shake with cracked ice; strain into chilled cocktail glass.

DEPTH BOMB

1 jigger applejack
1 jigger brandy
¼ teaspoon grenadine
¼ teaspoon lemon juice

Shake well with ice and strain into glass.

DIKI-DIKI (1)

⅔ Calvados or apple brandy
⅙ Swedish Punch
⅙ grapefruit juice

Stir well with ice and strain into glass.

DIKI-DIKI (2)

⅙ dry gin
⅙ grapefruit juice
⅔ applejack

Ice and shake.

FULL HOUSE

Dash of bitters
⅓ yellow Chartreuse
⅓ Benedictine
⅓ apple whiskey

Frank Scully's FUN IN BED COCKTAIL

1 part grape juice
1 apple whiskey

Ice, shake and serve.

GOLDEN DAWN

⅓ apple brandy
⅓ apricot brandy
⅓ dry gin
Dash of orange juice

Shake well, strain into cocktail glass; top with barspoon of grenadine, which will submarine to the bottom of the glass and there stage a sunrise effect.

JACK-IN-THE-BOX

1 jigger applejack
½ jigger pineapple juice
Juice of ½ lemon
2 dashes Angostura bitters

Shake well with ice and strain into glass.

JACK ROSE (1)

Juice of lime
⅓ grenadine syrup
⅔ applejack

JACK ROSE (2)

1 part grenadine
2 parts lemon juice
8 parts apple brandy

Shake vigorously with plenty of cracked or crushed ice and strain into chilled cocktail glasses. Twist of lemon.

JERSEY LIGHTNING

2 jiggers applejack
1 dash Angostura bitters
Sugar syrup to taste

Shake well with ice and strain into glass.

JERSEY MUG

Place in a heated mug 2 jiggers applejack, 1 good dash Angostura bitters, several whole cloves, and a large twist of lemon peel. Fill with boiling water and float applejack on top. Blaze and serve.

JERSEY SOUR

1 part simple syrup
2 parts lemon juice
8 parts apple brandy

Shake vigorously with plenty of cracked or crushed ice and strain into chilled cocktail glass. Decorate with cherry.

HONEYMOON

1 jigger applejack
½ jigger Benedictine
Juice of ½ lemon
3 dashes curaçao

Shake well with ice and strain into glass.

KENNY (FOR 4)

3 jiggers applejack
2 jiggers sweet vermouth
Juice of ½ lemon
1 dash Angostura bitters
2 dashes grenadine

Shake well with ice and strain into glasses.

KIDDIE CAR

1 part Triple Sec
2 parts lime juice
8 parts apple brandy

LIBERTY

⅔ applejack
⅓ light rum
1 dash sugar syrup

Shake well with ice and strain into glass.

MARCONI WIRELESS

2 dashes orange bitters
⅓ Italian vermouth
⅔ applejack

MOONLIGHT

2 or 3 jiggers Calvados or applejack
Juice of 1 lemon
1½ teaspoons sugar

Shake well with shaved ice and strain into tall glass. Fill with chilled soda water. Decorate with fruit if desired.

NEWTON'S APPLE COCKTAIL

2 hearty dashes Angostura bitters
1½ ounces apple brandy
½ ounce curaçao

Shake well with cracked ice, strain into chilled cocktail glass.

OOM PAUL

½ Calvados or apple brandy
½ Dubonnet
1 dash Angostura bitters

Stir well with ice and strain into glass.

PHILADELPHIA SCOTCHMAN

⅓ applejack
⅓ port
⅓ orange juice

Place in large cocktail glass with cracked ice and fill with soda water.

PRINCESS MARY'S PRIDE

½ Calvados or apple brandy
¼ Dubonnet
¼ dry vermouth

Stir well with ice and strain into glass.

ROULETTE

½ Calvados or apple brandy
¼ light rum
¼ Swedish Punch

Stir well with ice and strain into glass.

ROYAL SMILE

½ applejack
¼ dry gin
¼ grenadine
Juice of ¼ lemon

Shake well with ice and strain into glass.

SHARKY PUNCH

¾ Calvados or apple brandy
¼ rye whiskey
1 teaspoon sugar syrup

Shake well with ice and strain into glass. Add dash of soda water.

SPECIAL ROUGH

½ applejack
½ brandy
1 dash Pernod

Stir with shaved ice and strain into glass.

STONE FENCE

1 jigger apple brandy
2 dashes Angostura

Stir in tall glass with 2 ice cubes. Fill with cider.

TINTON

⅔ applejack
⅓ port wine

Stir well with ice and strain into glass.

TORPEDO

⅔ Calvados or apple brandy
⅓ brandy
1 dash gin

Stir well with ice and strain into glass.

TULIP

1/3 Calvados or apple brandy
1/3 sweet vermouth
1/6 apricot brandy
1/6 lemon juice

Stir well with ice and strain into glass.

WARDAY'S

1 teaspoon yellow Chartreuse
1/3 applejack
1/3 Italian vermouth
1/3 gin

BRANDY AND CORDIALS

AMABILE BEONE

(John Bruno, Pen & Pencil, New York)

In a 4 ounce brandy glass, put a dash of absinthe (Pernod) and roll it around so the liquid is distributed over the inside of the glass. Upend the glass in sugar to coat the rim. In a shaker, mix ⅓ Drambuie and ⅔ green crème de menthe and shake well with ice. *Sempre libera!*

ANGEL'S TIP

¾ crème de cacao
¼ cream

Pour carefully into liqueur glass, floating cream on top.

ANGEL'S WINGS

⅓ Crème de Violette
⅓ raspberry syrup
⅓ Maraschino

Pour ingredients carefully into liqueur glass so that they do not mix.

ANIS DEL OSO

1 glass Anis del Oso
1 glass grenadine
Soda water in tall glass

APRICOT COOLER

Park an 8-ounce glass filled two-thirds with finely cracked ice while you take a whole apricot, canned or fresh-stewed (not *you*, the apricot) with pit ousted, and put this fruit demolishingly through a coarse strainer, receiving it in a cocktail shaker, together with 1 jigger apricot brandy, ½ jigger lemon juice, 1 barspoon sugar.

Now empty ice from parked glass into shaker and do a thorough agitation job for 3 minutes.

Pour entire works, unstrained, into the chilled glass and serve with straw.

ARGENTINE JULEP

Into a tall 12-ouncer put

1 ounce each of orange and pineapple juices
1 ounce each of Spanish brandy and light claret
¼ ounce Cointreau

Frost with shaved ice; sprinkle ½ teaspoon sugar. Dress with orange slice and mint sprig.

AUNT JEMIMA

⅓ brandy
⅓ crème de cacao
⅓ Benedictine

Pour ingredients carefully into a liqueur glass so that they are in separate layers. Serve after dinner.

B & B

1 part cognac
1 part Benedictine

Mix, pour into liqueur glass and serve at room temperature.

BALTIMORE BRACER

1 ounce cognac
1 ounce anisette
1 egg white

Shake with cracked ice.

BENEDICTINE FRAPPE

Fill a large cocktail glass with shaved ice and fill with Benedictine. Serve after dinner with straws.

BETSY ROSS COCKTAIL

2 dashes Angostura bitters
1½ ounces brandy
1½ ounces port wine
Dash of curaçao.

Stir well in cracked ice, strain into large cocktail glass.

BETWEEN-SHEETS

⅓ cognac
⅓ crème de cacao
⅓ cream
1 dash bitters
1 teaspoon sugar
Lemon peel
Plenty cracked ice

Shake well, strain and serve.

BLACKBERRY COOLER

10-ounce glass filled two-thirds with cracked ice.
1 jigger (1½ ounces) blackberry brandy
½ ounce lemon juice
Sparkling water till high tide
Lemon slice and cherry as flotsam jetsam

Stir, serve with straw.

BLACKJACK

1 pony Kirsch
1 dash brandy
1 pony coffee

Frappéed with fine ice. Any of these will bring out the figure-skating-champ instincts in you.

BLANCHE

⅓ Cointreau
⅓ anisette
⅓ white curaçao

Shake well with ice and strain into glass.

BLUE TRAIN COCKTAIL

Shake well together with cracked ice, ¼ brandy and ¼ lightly sweetened pineapple juice. Fill glass ½ full with this mixture and fill with iced champagne.

BOMBAY

½ brandy
¼ sweet vermouth
¼ dry vermouth
2 dashes curaçao
1 dash Pernod

Stir well with ice and strain into glass.

BOMBER

1 jigger cognac
⅓ jigger Cointreau
⅓ jigger anisette
⅔ jigger vodka

Shake well with ice and strain into large glass.

BOSOM CARESSER

⅙ curaçao
⅙ brandy
⅓ madeira
1 teaspoon grenadine
1 yolk of egg

BRANDY BLAZER

2 jiggers brandy
1 small twist orange peel
1 twist lemon peel
1 lump sugar

Place sugar in bottom of shaker and add other ingredients. Stir with a long spoon; blaze for a few seconds and extinguish. Strain into glass. Serve after dinner.

BRANDY CHAMPARELLE

¼ curaçao
¼ yellow Chartreuse
¼ anisette
¼ brandy

BRANDY COCKTAIL (1)

1 jigger brandy
1 dash gin
1 dash bitters

BRANDY (2)

½ brandy
½ French vermouth
1 dash orange bitters

BRANDY CRUSTAS

(Harry's Bar, Paris)

Take small wine glass, moisten rim with lemon, dip rim of glass into castor sugar. Peel the rind of half a lemon and fit this curl of peel into the contour of your glass. Then in a shaker mix 1 teaspoon of sugar, 3 dashes of maraschino, 3 dashes of bitters, juice of one-quarter of a lemon, 1 glass of brandy. Shake well and pour into a prepared glass.

BRANDY COCKTAIL (3)

Cracked ice
1 sprig of mint
1 lemon peel, squeezing juice in glass
½ teaspoon sugar
1 drop bitters
½ teaspoon curaçao
2 ounces cognac

Shake lightly, strain, and serve in 10-ounce glass.

BRANDY DAISY

2 ounces brandy
½ ounce grenadine
Juice of 1 lemon

Shake with finely cracked ice;

pour unstrained into ample highball glass; decorate with fruits ad lid. Harpoon with straw.

BRANDY FIX

Dissolve one teaspoon of sugar in one teaspoon of water in small tumbler. Add juice of a half lemon, 1 jigger of brandy, ½ jigger cherry brandy, fill the glass with chipped ice, stir and serve with a straw.

BRANDY FIZZ

Juice of one lemon
1 barspoon sugar
1 jigger brandy
2 dashes yellow Chartreuse

Shake well with ice; strain; fill glass with carbonated water.

BRANDY FLIP

2 ounces brandy
1 dash bitters
½ teaspoon curaçao
1 sprig of mint
½ teaspoon sugar
Lemon peel

Shake well and strain.

BRANDY FLOAT

Place 1 or 2 cubes of ice in an Old Fashioned glass and fill it nearly full of chilled soda water. Lay the bowl of a teaspoon just at the top and pour in brandy carefully so that it flows out over the surface but does not mix. The amount of brandy is optional. Rum or any whiskey may be substituted for the brandy.

BRANDY MINT JULEP

3 jiggers cognac brandy
4 sprigs mint (uncrushed)
1 teaspoonful powdered sugar

Place mint in large glass, and then dissolve sugar. Add brandy and shaved ice. Stir well till very cold.

BRANDY PUNCH

Fill wineglass half full shaved ice
Add one teaspoon sugar
1 teaspoon pineapple juice
Juice of ¼ lemon
A few dashes of lime juice
1 large jigger brandy

Stir well, add a squirt of soda, serve with a dash of rum and fruit on top.

BRANDY SMASH

Muddle 1 lump of sugar with 1 ounce carbonated water and 4 sprigs of green mint. Add 2 ounces brandy, then a cube of ice. Stir and decorate with a slice of orange and a cherry. Twist lemon peel on top, using an Old Fashioned glass.

BRANDY SOUR

1½ ounces brandy
Juice of half a lemon
1 teaspoon sugar
1 to 3 dashes of Angostura

Shake with cracked ice. Strain into glass, preferably Delmonico. May be cargoed with orange slice and a cherry.

BRANT

¾ brandy
¼ white mint
2 dashes of bitters
1 piece of lemon peel

BROUSSARD'S ORANGE BRULOT

(*As served in the famous New Orleans restaurant*)

Cut a thin-skinned orange through skin around circumference, careful not to touch the fruit. With a teaspoon handle turn the skin back until it forms a cup. Do this on both ends and you have a peeled orange with a cup at each end. Place one cup on your plate. Pour some brandy into upper cup, put a lump of sugar in the brandy, light, stir gently as it burns, then drink it when the flame dies. (Brandy burns more easily if previously warmed; run hot water over the bottle before bringing to table.)

BULLDOG

1 jigger cherry brandy
½ light rum
Juice ½ lime

Shake well with ice and strain into glass.

BUTTON HOOK

¼ Pernod
¼ apricot brandy
¼ brandy
¼ white crème de menthe

Shake well with ice and strain into glass.

CAFE COCKTAIL

1 black coffee
½ crème de cacao
½ cognac
1 teaspoonful sugar
Lemon peel

Shake well, strain and serve.

CALEDONIA

⅓ crème de cacao
⅓ cognac
⅓ milk
Yolk of egg
1 dash bitters
Lemon peel

Shake well, strain, and serve with cinnamon on top.

CHAMPAGNE DES PAUVRES

1 glass of brandy
½ glass lemon syrup

CHARLES

½ brandy
½ sweet vermouth
1 dash Angostura or orange bitters

Stir well with ice and strain into glass.

CHARLIE CHAPLIN

3 ounces sloe gin
1 ounce lime juice
3 ounces apricot brandy

Shake over crushed ice.

CHICAGO

1 jigger brandy
1 dash curaçao
1 dash Angostura bitters

Stir well with ice and strain into glass frosted with sugar. Fill with iced champagne.

CITY SLICKER

⅔ brandy
⅓ curaçao

Shake well with ice and strain into glass.

CLASSIC

½ brandy
⅙ curaçao
⅙ Maraschino
⅙ lemon juice

Stir well with ice and strain.

COFFEE COCKTAIL

1 pony of brandy
2 ponies of port
1 egg yolk
¼ teaspoon sugar

Serve in claret glass.

COLD DECK

1 dash Pernod
½ brandy
¼ sweet vermouth
¼ white crème de menthe

Stir well with ice and strain into glass.

COPENHAGEN SPECIAL

(Copenhagen Restaurant, New York City)

In a mixing glass with plenty of crushed ice, shake 1 part each of Aquavit, Arrack punch and fresh lemon juice. Serve in chilled cocktail glass.

CREME DE CACAO, CREAM FLOAT

Gently pour 1 teaspoon heavy cream onto crème de cacao in liqueur glass. Serve without stirring, the cream a clean layer on top.

CUBAN COCKTAIL

⅔ brandy
⅓ apricot brandy
Juice of one-half lime

THE DEVIL

⅔ jigger brandy
⅓ jigger green créme de menthe
1 pinch red pepper

Shake brandy and crème de menthe and strain into glass. Sprinkle red pepper on top.

DIANA

¾ white crème de menthe
¼ brandy
Shaved ice

Place ice in glass and pour in crème de menthe. Top carefully with the brandy.

THE DOBBS

(Dick's Cabin, Dobbs Ferry, N. Y.)

Pour white crème de menthe over crushed ice in a broad-flange cocktail glass until near top. Then flirt across the ice, several dashes of Fernet Branca.

DOLORES

1/3 cherry brandy
1/3 crème de cacao
1/3 Spanish brandy
White of one egg

DOUBLE ARROW

1/2 light curaçao
1/2 Crème d'Yvette
Cream

Pour carefully into liqueur glasses so that liqueurs do not mix, and top with cream.

DREAM

1/3 curaçao
2/3 brandy
Dash absinthe

DUCHESS

1/3 Pernod
1/3 dry vermouth
1/3 sweet vermouth

Shake well with ice and strain into glass.

EAST INDIA COCKTAIL (1)

1 teaspoon of curaçao
1 teaspoon pineapple syrup
1 jigger brandy
2 dashes bitters

Stir with spoon, serve with cherry in cocktail glass.

EAST INDIA COCKTAIL (2)

1 1/2 ounces brandy
1 teaspoon pineapple juice
1 teaspoon curaçao, preferably the red
3 dashes Angostura

Ice and shake; strain onto a cherry.

EGG LEMONADE

Fill your shaker half full chopped ice, add 1 fresh egg, 1 teaspoon sugar, juice of 1 lemon, 1 jigger of brandy. Shake well, strain into large glass and fill with soda.

EGG SOUR

1 jigger brandy
1 jigger curaçao
Juice of 1/2 lemon
1 egg
1 teaspoon sugar

Shake well with ice and strain into Delmonico glass.

FRENCH VERMOUTH AND CURACAO

1 glass French vermouth
1/2 glass curaçao
Soda water

GEORGE'S BEAUTY

(for a morning pick-up)

Juice of 1/2 lemon, freshly squeezed
Generous jigger of good brandy
White of 1 egg
Teaspoon of bar sugar

Shake thoroughly, strain into a highball glass and fill with soda.

GLAD EYE

2/3 Pernod
1/3 peppermint

Shake well with ice and strain into glass.

GLOOM CHASER

¼ Grand Marnier
¼ curaçao
¼ lemon juice
¼ grenadine

Stir well with ice and strain into glass.

GOLDEN DRAGON

(Stonehenge, Ridgefield, Connecticut)

Float ¼ ounce good French brandy over ¾ ounce yellow Chartreuse

Serve in brandy cordial glass.

GRASSHOPPER

⅓ crème de cacao
⅓ green crème de menthe
⅓ light sweet cream

Shake until very cold, serve in cordial glass.

GREEN DRAGON

(Stonehenge, Ridgefield Connecticut)

Float ¼ ounce good French brandy over ¾ ounce green Chartreuse

Serve in brandy cordial glass.

GRENADIER

⅔ brandy
⅓ ginger brandy
1 dash Jamaica ginger
1 teaspoon powdered sugar

Stir well with ice and strain into glass.

HABITANT COCKTAIL

(Château Frontenac, Quebec, Canada)

Shake with ice cubes

1½ ounces cognac
½ ounce fresh lemon juice
½ ounce maple syrup

Serve very cold, decorate with cherry.

HARVARD

Dash of orange bitters
⅖ jigger brandy
⅗ Italian vermouth (stir)

Fill with soda water.

HOOP LA

¼ brandy
¼ lemon juice
¼ Cointreau
¼ Lillet

Stir well with ice and strain into glass.

HOP FROG

⅓ brandy
⅔ lime juice

Ice and shake.

JAPANESE

1 jigger of brandy
2 dashes Orgeat syrup
1 slice lemon peel

THE JOHNSON DELIGHT

⅔ Pernod
½ Cointreau
Juice of ½ lime

Shake well and strain over cracked ice in Old Fashioned

glass. Repeat often as desired, facing east.

KIRSCH AND CASSIS

1 glass Cassis
½ glass Kirsch
Balance, soda water

KISS-ME-QUICK HIGHBALL

2 dashes Angostura bitters
1½ ounces Pernod
4 dashes curaçao

Shake well with cracked ice and strain into an 8-ounce highball glass. Add additional ice and carbonated water to fill. Stir slightly.

KISS THE BOYS GOODBYE

½ sloe gin
½ brandy
½ white of egg
Juice of 1 lemon

Shake very well with plenty of ice and strain.

LADY BE GOOD

½ brandy
¼ white crème de menthe
¼ sweet vermouth

Shake with cracked ice and strain into glass.

Burl Ives' LALLAH ROOKH COCKTAIL

In a shaker, chill a jigger of cognac with ½ jigger dark Barbados rum, 1 teaspoon thick cream, 1½ teaspoon sugar, pony of vanilla extract. Strain into cocktail glass with hollow stem.

LAYER CAKE

⅓ crème de cacao
⅓ apricot brandy
⅓ cream

Pour carefully into liqueur glass so that ingredients do not mix. Place cherry on top. Chill mixture in glass.

LIEBFRAUMILCH

1 jigger crème de cacao
1 jigger cream
Juice of 1 lime

Shake well with ice and strain into glass.

LIL NAUE

⅓ cognac
⅓ port wine
⅓ apricot brandy
1 teaspoon sugar
1 lemon peel
Yolk of egg

Shake well with cracked ice and serve with cinnamon on top.

LIZARD SKIN

Hollow out half of a large orange. Pour in large jigger brandy. Light flame, extinguish after a moment, then drink.

LOVERS DELIGHT

1 ounce Cointreau
1 ounce Forbidden Fruit
1 ounce cognac

Shake.

LUGGER

½ brandy
½ Calvados or apple brandy
1 dash apricot brandy

Stir with ice and strain into glass. Serve with twist of orange peel.

MACKINNON

1 jigger Drambuie
¼ jigger light rum
Juice ½ lime
Juice ¼ lemon

Shake well. Serve in tall glass with plenty of ice and add seltzer.

MAIDEN'S KISS

⅕ Crème de Roses
⅕ curaçao
⅕ Maraschino
⅕ yellow Chartreuse
⅕ Benedictine

MANANA

1 part lemon juice
1 part grenadine
2 parts apricot brandy
6 parts light rum

Shake with finely crushed ice and strain into cocktail glass.

MERRY WIDOW

½ cherry brandy
½ Maraschino

Shake well with ice and serve with a cherry.

METROPOLITAN

½ brandy
½ sweet vermouth
2 dashes sugar syrup
1 dash Angostura bitters

Stir well with ice and strain into glass.

MIKADO

1 jigger brandy
2 dashes curaçao
2 dashes Orgeat syrup
2 dashes Crème de Noyau
2 dashes Angostura bitters

Stir well with ice and strain into glass.

MONTANA

1 part French vermouth
1 part port wine
4 parts cognac

Stir with cubes, and serve in cocktail glass which has been prechilled.

MORNING AFTER

1 white of egg
1 teaspoonful anisette syrup
1 glass absinthe
Dash of soda on top

Rise Stevens' MORNING GLORY

Fill Collins glass with ice chunks, pour ½ ounce Cointreau, ½ ounce cherry brandy, dash of Angostura bitters. Add orange, pineapple slices. Fill with champagne.

MY SIN COCKTAIL

1 ounce absinthe
1 ounce anisette

1 drop bitters
White of egg

Plenty of ice, shake well and strain.

NETHERLAND

⅔ brandy
⅓ curaçao
1 dash orange bitters

NETHERLAND COCKTAIL (2)

1 ounce brandy
1 ounce curaçao
Dash orange bitters

Stir amid cracked ice. Strain.

THE NICOLOSCAR

Take a thin slice of lemon, trimming edge rind away with sharp knife. Place on this lemon slice (à la hors d'oeuvre) coarse-grind coffee, equal amount of coarse-grain sugar, covering the slice. In a brandy snifter, place 1½ ounces of fine cognac. Put the laden lemon slice in your mouth, chew vigorously, and wash the entire thing down with the brandy.

NIGHT CAP

Beat yolk of a fresh egg, add one pony of anisette, one pony orange curaçao, one pony of brandy. Add hot water and leave a call for 2 o'clock.

NUGENT

⅔ Calvados
⅙ Swedish Punch
⅙ grapefruit juice

O'HEARN SPECIAL

2 jiggers brandy
1 twist orange peel
2 sprigs mint

Place in tall glass with ice cubes. Fill up with ginger ale. Stir and serve.

PANSY

1 jigger Pernod
6 dashes grenadine
2 dashes Angostura bitters

Shake well with ice and strain into glass.

PARADISE

⅓ apricot brandy
⅓ dry gin
⅓ orange juice
Dash of lime juice

Ice and shake will.

Jane Pickens'
PICKENS' PUNCH

⅓ peach brandy
⅓ cherry liqueur
⅓ crème de menthe

Shake, then let stand for five minutes. Serve without ice.

PICK-ME-UP

½ Dubonnet
½ cognac
⅓ anisette
Lemon peel
White of egg
Cracked ice

Shake well, strain and be picked up.

PICON GRENADINE

1 jigger Amer Picon
½ jigger grenadine

Place with ice cubes in Old-Fashioned glass and fill with soda water.

PISCO PUNCH

In a large wineglass or small tumbler place 1 piece of ice with a teaspoon each of pineapple and lemon juice. Add 2 jiggers brandy, a small cube of pineapple and fill with cold water. Stir well and serve.

POOPDECK

½ brandy
¼ port
¼ blackberry brandy

Shake well with ice and strain into glass.

POUSSE CAFE (1)

⅙ grenadine
⅙ Maraschino
⅙ green crème de menthe
⅙ Crème de Violette
⅙ Chartreuse
⅙ brandy

Add carefully in order given to keep each liqueur separate.

POUSSE CAFE (2)

⅙ Maraschino
⅙ raspberry syrup
⅙ crème de cacao
⅙ curaçao
⅙ Chartreuse
⅙ brandy

(The trick is to pour these slowly, one by one, into a liqueur glass so that the colors stay in their strata. This is not governed by law, but specific gravity. You can choose your own colors.) And in the good old summertime, when an ordinary cordial seems forbiddingly heavy, flavor-cravers will favor: *Iced Crème de Café* (rich coffee liqueur, one jigger thereof, in glass of shaved ice, filled up with fizz and topped with sweet cream). And *Iced Crème de Cacao* (voluptuous chocolate liqueur with vanilla aura, similarly coolerized). And short-strawed fragrant verdant *Menthe Frappé* (crème de menthe liqueur shaved-iced in a cocktail glass). And *Apricot Delight* (1 part each of orange and lemon juices, 2 parts apricot brandy, ice-shaken and strained). And *Pernod Highball* (famous legal version of absinthe, now made in America, fizzed and cubed). And cetera.

POUSSE L'AMOUR

⅓ Maraschino
Drop in 1 yolk of egg
⅓ crème vanilla
⅓ brandy

Egg yolk must not run into the liqueur

PRESTO

⅔ brandy
⅓ sweet vermouth

1 dash orange juice
1 dash Pernod

Stir well with ice and strain into glass.

PRINCE OF WALES

1 dash Angostura bitters
1 teaspoon curaçao
½ jigger madeira
½ jigger brandy

Place in shaker with ice and shake thoroughly. Strain into wineglass, fill with iced champagne and decorate with cherry and slice of orange.

PUMPKIN COACH COCKTAIL

2 parts liqueur Cesoriac
1 part vermouth
1 part cherry juice
3 limes (to each pint)

Slathers of ice (or you will go home in a basket).

QUEEN ELIZABETH (1)

½ brandy
½ sweet vermouth
1 dash curaçao

Stir well with ice and strain into glass. Add a cherry if desired.

QUEEN ELIZABETH (2)

¼ Benedictine
½ French vermouth
¼ lime juice

QUEEN'S PICK

Pour in 1 jigger brandy over 1 ice cube in large wineglass. Then fill with champagne.

QUELLE VIE COCKTAIL

⅓ Kümmel
⅔ brandy

RAINBOW

1/7 yellow Chartreuse
1/7 green Chartreuse
1/7 crème de cacao
1/7 Crème de Violette
1/7 Maraschino
1/7 Benedictine
1/7 brandy

Pour ingredients carefully into large liqueur glass so that they do not mix. Serve only after dinner.

RHETT BUTLER

1 jigger Southern Comfort
Juice of ¼ lime
Juice of ¼ lemon
1 teaspoon curaçao
½ teaspoon powdered sugar

Shake well with ice and strain into glass.

ROLLS ROYCE COCKTAIL

½ ounce cognac
½ ounce Cointreau
½ ounce orange juice

Shake with cracked ice; strain into chilled cocktail glass.

SAUCY SUE

½ brandy
½ Calvados or apple brandy
1 dash apricot brandy
1 dash Pernod

Stir well with ice and strain

into glass. Squeeze orange peel over top.

SAVOY HOTEL

⅓ brandy
⅓ Benedictine
⅓ crème de cacao

Pour ingredients carefully into liqueur glass so that they do not mix. Serve after dinner.

SCARLETT O'HARA

1½ jiggers Southern Comfort
1½ jiggers cranberry juice
Juice of ¼ lime

Stir well with ice and strain into glass.

SCHUSSBOOMER'S DELIGHT

(Sun Valley Lodge, Sun Valley, Idaho)

Place 2 ice cubes, ¾ ounce fresh lemon juice, and 1½ ounces cognac in Tom Collins glass. Fill with champagne.

SIDECAR (1)

⅔ brandy
⅓ Cointreau
Dash of lime juice

Shake with very fine ice; strain into frosty cocktail glass.

SIDECAR (2)

(50 Million Frenchmen . . .)

⅓ lemon juice
⅓ Cointreau
⅓ cognac

Shake with cracked ice; strain.

SINK OR SWIM

¾ brandy
¼ sweet vermouth
1 dash Angostura bitters

Stir well with ice and strain into glass.

SLEDGE HAMMER

⅓ brandy
⅓ rum
⅓ apple brandy
1 dash Pernod

Shake well with ice and strain into glass.

SLEEPY HEAD

2 jiggers brandy
1 twist orange peel
4 leaves fresh mint, slightly crushed
1-2 cubes ice

SNOWBALL

⅙ Crème de Violette
⅙ white crème de menthe
⅙ anisette
⅙ fresh cream
⅓ gin

SOUTH AFRICAN "SUNDOWNER"

(Recipe in use nearly 300 years.)

⅕ orange juice
⅕ lemon juice
⅕ Van der Hum liqueur
⅖ Cape of Good Hope brandy

Stir with ice; serve in sizable cocktail glass.

STARS AND STRIPES

1/3 green Chartreuse
1/3 Maraschino
1/3 Crème de Cassis

Pour carefully into liqueur glass so that ingredients do not mix. Serve after dinner.

STINGER (1)

2 parts brandy
1 part white crème de menthe

Stir with cracked ice in tall mixing glass; strain into cocktail glass. The Stinger is sometimes served with a pair of short straws.

STINGER (2)

(The Colony Restaurant, New York City)

Shake with cracked ice 1 ounce white crème de menthe and 2 ounces of cognac. Strain into chilled cocktail glass and serve.

STIRRUP CUP (1)

(The Chase Hotel, St. Louis, Missouri)

Mix 1 jigger cranberry juice with 1 teaspoon fresh lemon juice in a double Old-Fashioned glass. Add 1 jigger Southern Comfort. Fill glass with ice cubes, grapefruit juice, and soda. Decorate with mint.

STIRRUP CUP (2)

1 jigger cherry brandy
1 jigger brandy
Juice of half lemon

(Attributed, but not by me, to George Washington).

TANTALUS

1/3 brandy
1/3 Forbidden Fruit liqueur
1/3 lemon juice

Shake well with ice and strain into glass.

TEMPTER

1/2 apricot brandy
1/2 port

Stir well with ice and strain into glass.

TENDER

1/4 apricot brandy
1/4 apple brandy
1/2 gin
1 dash lemon juice

Shake well with ice and strain into glass.

Morley Callaghan's THEY SHALL INHERIT THE EARTH COCKTAIL

2 parts brandy
2 parts lemon juice
1 part Cointreau
1 part Benedictine

THUNDER

2 jiggers brandy
1 teaspoon sugar syrup
1 egg yolk
1 pinch cayenne pepper

Shake well with ice and strain into glass.

TIN WEDDING

¾ jigger brandy
¾ dry gin
¾ sweet vermouth
2 dashes orange bitters

Shake well with ice and strain into glass.

TOMATE

2 jiggers absinthe
1 jigger spring water
1 teaspoon grenadine syrup

Shake with shaved ice or frappé in mixer. Pour into cocktail glass and decorate with twist of lemon peel.

TRIPLICE

⅓ Benedictine
⅓ French vermouth
⅓ gin

TROPICAL COCKTAIL

1 dash of bitters
1 dash of orange bitters
⅓ crème de cacao
⅓ Maraschino
⅓ French vermouth

ULYSSES

⅓ cherry brandy
⅓ French vermouth
⅓ brandy

Squeeze orange peel on top.

VALENCIA

⅔ apricot brandy
⅓ orange juice
2 dashes orange bitters

Stuart Cloete's VAN DER HUM

10 bottles of good brandy
20 tablespoons of finely cut naartjie (tangerine) peel, which should be free of all pith
10 dessert spoons cinnamon
50 cloves
½ nutmeg
A few cardamon seeds
1 handful orange blossoms

Mix the above ingredients with the brandy and leave for one month in a cask or demijohn, shaking every day. The vessel should be completely airtight. After one month strain off the spices, peel, etc., and add a cold thick syrup in the proportion of one cup of syrup to two of the brandy. Add one wineglass of best rum to every bottle of the Van der Hum. Leave in well-corked receptacle for at least a fortnight, shaking daily. Clarify, bottle and seal.

VICTORY

½ Pernod
½ grenadine

Shake well with ice and strain into glass. Fill with soda water.

WAGON WHEEL

1 part grenadine
2 parts lemon juice
3 parts cognac
5 parts Southern Comfort

Shake with cracked ice.

WEDDING BELLS

1/6 cherry brandy
1/6 orange juice
1/3 gin
1/3 Dubonnet

WHIP

1/2 brandy
1/4 sweet vermouth
1/4 dry vermouth
3 dashes curaçao
1 dash Pernod

WHITE LADY

2/3 Cointreau
1/6 crème de menthe
1/6 brandy

WIDOW'S DREAM

2 jiggers Benedictine
1 egg
1 jigger cream

Shake well with ice and strain into glass.

WIDOW'S KISS

1/4 Parfait D'Amour
1/4 yellow Chartreuse
1/4 Benedictine
White of egg floated on top

WILLIAM OF ORANGE

2/3 brandy
1/3 curaçao
1/3 orange bitters

Stir well with ice and strain into glass.

YELLOW PARROT

1/3 apricot brandy
1/3 yellow Chartreuse
1/3 Pernod

Shake well with ice and strain into glass.

XANTHIA

1/3 cherry brandy
1/3 yellow Chartreuse
1/3 gin

Frozen Blender Drinks

APPLEJACK FLIP
(Serves 2)

2⅔ jiggers applejack
1 egg
2 teaspoons sugar
½ cup shaved ice

Chill all ingredients and place in chilled container of electric blender. Cover and blend for 20 seconds. Pour into 6-ounce glasses and sprinkle with nutmeg.

BATH CURE
(Pump Room, Chicago, Ill.)

Fill an electric mixer ¼ full of cracked ice and add ½ ounce grenadine, 1 ounce each lemon, pineapple and orange juice, ½ ounce lime juice, 1½ ounces Jamaica rum, 1 ounce Puerto Rican gold rum, 2 ounces light rum, 1 ounce 151-proof rum, 1½ ounces brandy, 1½ ounces vodka. Pour into 14-ounce glass that has been set in a mold of shaved ice. Add fruit and decorate ice mold with red and green liquids.

BLOODY MARY
(Serves 4)

Into your blender glass put:

8 ounces tomato juice
3 ounces vodka
Juice of two lemons
White of one egg
½ teaspoon salt
Freshly ground pepper
2 fresh celery leaves (or ¼ teaspoon dried celery flakes)
4 dashes Lea and Perrin Worcestershire sauce
1 cup cracked ice

Blend ingredients for about one minute or until ice is completely mixed.

BOURBON SOUR
(Hotel Mark Hopkins, San Francisco)

Time is the essence of the drink as served here. Shake *not over 15 seconds* in electric mixer: small scoop cracked ice, 1⅛ ounces each fresh lemon juice and whiskey, one teaspoon bar sugar. Serve in 6-ounce sour glass with maraschino cherry.

BRANDY FLIP
(The Drake's Camellia House, Chicago, Illinois)

Into electric mixer put shaved ice, 1¼ ounces brandy, 1 whole egg, ½ teaspoon sugar. Mix at high speed. Pour into 6½ ounce champagne cocktail glass. Sprinkle with nutmeg.

COCKTAIL A LA NOIX DE COCO
(Serves 4)

This cocktail originated in the French West Indies. The ingredients were entrusted to the skillful hands of the natives who are born cooks with a heaven-sent gift for perfect blending.

Milk from one coconut
2 wineglasses of brandy
2 wineglasses Maraschino
½ teaspoon Angostura bitters
1 cup crushed ice

Blend ingredients about one minute or until ice is completely mixed.

COMMODORE

⅓ bourbon whiskey
⅓ crème de cacao
⅓ lemon juice

Dash of grenadine syrup, serve in champagne glass. Tradition can be improved by the use of an electric mixer, with the resultant ice-floe similar to that of a Frozen Daiquiri.

DIXIE PUNCH

½ jigger gin
1 jigger Southern Comfort
½ jigger lime juice
2 dashes grenadine
½ slice pineapple

Mix drastically in an electric mixer, without ice. Then pour onto shaved ice in a Mint Julep goblet or Collins glass, decorated with pineapple and slice of orange.

FLORIDITA SPECIAL
(Serves 4)

Put into your blender glass:

4 ounces rum
2 level teaspoons granulated sugar
2 teaspoons grapefruit juice
2 teaspoons Maraschino liqueur
Juice of 1 medium lime
3 cups of finely cracked ice

It is extremely important not to alter the order of the ingredients. Chill your cocktail glasses by pouring in cracked ice and a little water. Now you're ready to freeze-spin your Floridita Special. Hold on the top of the blender and turn to *high speed.* Blend ingredients for about 20 seconds. This requires careful watching. This drink, when perfect, should be the consistency of lightly frozen sherbet.

GRAPE-VODKA FROTH

(Serves 4)

Put into your blender glass:

3 ounces vodka
8 ounces grape juice
Juice of ½ lemon
White of one egg
1 cup cracked ice

Blend on high speed about one and a half minutes and pour into chilled cocktail glasses.

LADY HOPKINS

(Hotel Mark Hopkins, San Francisco, California)

In electric mixer, jigger Southern Comfort, ⅔ jigger passion fruit, juice ¼ lime, dash of bottled unsweetened lime juice. Pour into iced glass. Add mint, cherry and orange.

SCORPION

(Trader Vic's, Oakland, California)

Into electric mixer, put 2 ounces orange juice, 1½ ounces lemon juice, 2 ounces light Puerto Rican rum, 1 ounce brandy, ½ ounce orgeat syrup, and half a scoop shaved ice. Pour into Grapefruit Supreme glass, decorate with orange slice.

SHERRY FLIP

(Pump Room, Ambassador East, Chicago, Ill.)

In your electric mixer: 1½ ounces sherry, ½ cup shaved ice, 1 heaping teaspoon granulated sugar, 1 whole egg (*sans* shell), 3 dashes crème de cacao. Mix well. Pour into well-chilled 5½ ounce champagne cocktail glass. Top with two or three pinches of nutmeg.

SPICED APPLEJACK CIDER

2 Old Fashioned-glass measures sweet cider
3 ounces applejack
½ teaspoon ground cinnamon
¼ teaspoon ground cloves
1 small whole orange (seedless and cut into 8 sections)
1 cup crushed ice

Blend on high speed about one minute and pour into chilled Old-Fashioned glasses.

TOMATE

2 jiggers absinthe
1 jigger spring water
1 teaspoon grenadine

Shake well with shaved ice or frappé in mixer. Pour into cocktail glass and decorate with twist of lemon peel.

TONGA

(Trader Vic's, San Francisco)

In blender, with half-scoop shaved ice, mix 1½ ounces fresh orange juice, ¾ ounce fresh lemon juice, 2½ ounces light rum, juice ½ lime, ¼ ounce curaçao, dash each grenadine and Jamaica rum. Serve in 14-ounce chimney glass. Decorate.

TOPPER COCKTAIL

(Winston Theatre Grill, Toronto, Canada)

Over the border it's the Topper; in an electric mixer, shuffle 1 small scoop of vanilla ice cream with ¼ ounce green crème de menthe and 1 ounce cognac. Simply serve in well-chilled champagne glass.

GIN

ABBEY COCKTAIL

2 dashes Angostura bitters
1½ ounces dry gin
¾ ounce orange juice
Generous dash sweet vermouth

Shake well with cracked ice and strain into cocktail glass. Add a maraschino cherry.

ADAM AND EVE

1 ounce Forbidden Fruit
1 ounce gin
1 ounce cognac
Dash of lemon juice

Shake over ice, and serve in chilled cocktail glass.

ALASKA

¾ dry gin
¼ yellow Chartreuse
2 dashes orange bitters

Stir well with ice and strain into glass. Serve with a twist of lemon peel.

ALEXANDER

⅓ gin
⅓ crème de cacao
⅓ cream

ALFONSO SPECIAL

¼ dry gin
¼ dry vermouth
½ Grand Marnier
4 dashes sweet vermouth
1 dash Angostura bitters

Shake well with ice and strain into glass.

ANGEL FACE

⅓ dry gin
⅓ apricot brandy
⅓ Calvados or apple brandy

Stir well with ice and strain into glass.

ANGLER'S COCKTAIL

2 dashes Angostura bitters
3 dashes orange bitters
1½ ounces dry gin
1 dash grenadine

Place ingredients in mixing glass with lump of ice. Stir vigorously, strain into Delmonico glass partly filled with cracked ice.

APPENDECTOMY

1 part Grand Marnier
2 parts lime juice

8 parts gin
1 egg white to each 2 drinks

Follow Appendicitis directions as to mixing.

APPENDICITIS

1 part curaçao
2 parts lemon juice
8 parts gin
1 whole egg to each 4 drinks

Put all ingredients except the gin in the shaker with cracked ice. Shake vigorously until thoroughly blended. Add ¼ of the gin and combine, then add balance ¼ at a time. Strain into cocktail glass, prechilled.

ARTILLERY

⅔ dry gin
⅓ sweet vermouth
2 dashes Angostura bitters

Stir well with ice and strain into glass. Serve with a twist of lemon peel.

ASTORIA

⅔ dry gin
⅓ dry vermouth
1 dash orange bitters

Stir well with ice and strain into glass. Serve with an olive.

William Seabrook's ASYLUM COCKTAIL

1 part gin
1 part Pernod
Dash of grenadine

Pour over large lumps of ice. Do not shake.

ATTENTION

¼ dry gin
¼ Pernod
¼ dry vermouth
¼ Crème de Violette
2 dashes orange bitters

Stir well with ice and strain into glass.

AVIATION

1 part Maraschino
2 parts lemon juice
8 parts gin

Shake vigorously with cracked ice.

B.V.D.

⅓ dry gin
⅓ light rum
⅓ dry vermouth

Stir well with ice and strain into glass.

BARBARY COAST

¼ dry gin
¼ Scotch whisky
¼ crème de cacao
¼ cream

Shake well with ice and strain into small highball or Old-Fashioned glass.

BARON

⅔ dry gin
⅓ dry vermouth
6 dashes curaçao
2 dashes sweet vermouth

Stir well with ice and strain into glass. Serve with a twist of lemon peel.

BEAUTY SPOT

⅔ gin
⅓ Grenadine
1 egg white

Shake well with ice and strain into glass.

BEE'S KNEES

1 part honey
2 parts lemon juice
8 parts gin

Shake vigorously with cracked ice.

BELMONT

⅔ gin
⅓ grenadine or raspberry syrup
½ jigger cream

Shake well with ice and strain into glass.

BERMUDA HIGHBALL

¾ jigger dry gin
¾ jigger brandy
½ jigger dry vermouth

Combine ingredients in highball glass, with ice cubes, and fill with ginger ale or soda water. Garnish with lemon peel and serve.

BERMUDA ROSE

1 jigger dry gin
1 dash grenadine
1 dash apricot brandy
⅓ jigger lemon or lime juice

Shake well with ice and strain into glass.

BIJOU

⅓ dry gin
⅓ green Chartreuse
⅓ sweet vermouth
1 dash orange bitters

Stir well with ice and strain into glass. Serve with a twist of lemon peel.

BLACKTHORN

⅔ sloe gin
⅓ Italian vermouth
Dash of Angostura
Twist of lemon peel, or dash of lemon juice

Stir with ice; strain into cocktail glass.

BLOODHOUND

½ dry gin
¼ dry vermouth
¼ sweet vermouth
2-3 crushed strawberries

Stir well with ice and strain into glass.

THE BLOWTORCH

(The Meadows Inn, Valhalla, N. Y.)

3 ounces Southern Comfort
3 ounces gin
3 ounces Triple Sec
3 ounces orange juice
1 ounce grenadine

Shake well with cracked ice. Pour into tall glass. Garnish with a blast from a blowtorch.

BLUE BIRD

2 jiggers dry gin
4 dashes Angostura bitters
4 dashes curaçao

Stir well with ice and strain into glass. Twist lemon peel over top and serve with a cherry.

BLUE DEVIL

1 part Parfait d'Amour
2 parts lemon juice
8 parts gin

Strain the lemon juice removing all pulp. Stir ingredients with large ice cubes.

BLUE MOON

⅔ gin
⅓ French vermouth
1 dash orange bitters
1 dash of Crème d'Yvette

BOOMERANG

1 ounce dry vermouth
2 ounces dry gin
1 dash Angostura bitters
2 dashes Maraschino

Stir and serve with lemon twist.

BOXCAR

½ pony Cointreau
1 jigger gin
Juice ½ lime
White of 1 egg
1 dash grenadine

Shake and strain into wineglass whose rim has been sugarfrosted.

BRONX

⅔ gin
⅓ orange juice
2 slices fresh pineapple in glass

CABARET

½ dry gin
½ Dubonnet
1 dash Pernod
1 dash Angostura bitters

Stir well with ice and strain into glass. Serve with a cherry.

CAFE DE PARIS

2 jiggers dry gin
3 dashes anisette
1 teaspoon cream
1 egg white

Shake well with ice and strain into glass.

CAMPDEN

½ dry gin
¼ Cointreau
¼ Lillet

Stir well with ice and strain into glass. Serve with a cherry.

CARUSO

⅓ dry gin
⅓ dry vermouth
⅓ green crème de menthe

Stir well with ice and strain into glass.

CASINO (I)

2 jiggers Old Tom gin
2 dashes Maraschino
2 dashes orange bitters
2 dashes lemon juice

Stir well with ice and strain into glass.

CASINO (2)

1 part Maraschino
1 part orange juice
1 part lemon juice
8 parts gin

Shake vigorously with cracked ice.

CHARLESTON

1/6 dry gin
1/6 Kirsch
1/6 Maraschino
1/6 curaçao
1/6 dry vermouth
1/6 sweet vermouth

Stir well with ice and strain into glass. Squeeze lemon peel over top.

CHERRY JULEP

1½ ounces dry gin
1 ounce sloe gin
1 ounce cherry brandy
1 teaspoon maraschino cherry syrup and 2 or 3 muddled cherries
Juice of one-half lemon
1 teaspoon sugar

Stir well, pour into 12-ounce glass, add cracked ice, and fill glass with seltzer. Garnish with one-half slice of lemon or orange, if desired as a color effect for the aesthetically-inclined.

CHINA CLIPPER COCKTAIL

Conspicuous passenger:
1 Chinese golden lime
(These kumquats, preserved in syrup and put up in earthenware jugs, are obtainable at any Chinese shop or restaurant.)

2/3 gin (yellow dry gin jibes best with the color scheme)
1/6 dry vermouth
1/6 grapefruit juice
2 shots orange bitters
1 or 2 drops of the syrup of the kumquat

The liquid ingredients are stirred in a mixing glass with ice cubes and poured onto Miss Golden Lime, already in her glass cabin. Pleasant take-off!

CHOCOLATE SOLDIER

1/3 Dubonnet
2/3 gin
Dash of lime juice

CLOVER CLUB (1)

(Bellevue-Stratford Hotel, Philadelphia, Pennsylvania)

Shake well juice of ½ lemon, 4 dashes grenadine, 2 ounces gin, white of 1 egg with ice. Strain into chilled cocktail glass.

CLOVER CLUB (2)

Juice ½ lemon
½ spoon sugar
½ pony raspberry syrup
¼ pony white of egg
1 jigger gin

CLOVER LEAF

1 part grenadine
2 parts lemon juice
8 parts gin
½ egg white

Float small sprig of mint on top.

THE CONNECTICUT BULLFROG

This cocktail must never be served on shore but always on a boat, provided that the boat is not over 45 feet long and the owner is the skipper (no hired hand). The ingredients are awful but the result does have something. Here they are and you must have them on board:

4 parts gin
1 part New England rum
1 part lemon juice
1 part maple syrup

Shake these ingredients together until your arms ache. Then have someone else do the same thing with about ten times the usual amount of ice. Serve frappé and regardless of the size or previous condition of servitude of your boat, all your guests will gratefully swear that they are at the Waldorf-Astoria at sea!

CORNELL (1)

1 jigger dry gin
3 dashes Maraschino
1 egg white

Shake well with ice and strain into glass.

CORNELL (2)

½ French vermouth
½ gin

Manuel Komroff's CORONET COCKTAIL

2 parts gin
1 part port wine

Stir with ice and peel of lemon.

COUNT CURREY

1 jigger of gin
1 spoon of sugar
2 cubes of ice

Put in a highball glass and fill with champagne.

DARBY

1 jigger dry gin
⅓ jigger lime juice
⅓ jigger grapefruit juice
1 teaspoon powdered sugar

Shake well with ice and strain into a large cocktail glass. Top with a squirt of soda and add a cherry.

DEEP SEA

½ Old Tom gin
½ dry vermouth
1 dash Pernod
1 dash orange bitters

Stir well with ice and strain into glass. Squeeze lemon peel over top and serve with an olive.

DELMONICO (1)

¾ ounce gin
½ ounce of French vermouth
½ ounce Italian vermouth
½ ounce cognac
2 dashes Angostura
Twist of orange peel

DELMONICO (2)

Dash of orange bitters
½ French vermouth
½ gin
2 slices orange peel

DEWEY

Dash of orange bitters
½ gin
½ French vermouth

DIXIE

½ jigger dry gin
¼ jigger Pernod
¼ jigger dry vermouth
Juice of ¼ orange
2 dashes grenadine

Shake well with ice and strai. into glass.

DIXIE PUNCH

½ jigger gin
1 jigger Southern Comfort
½ jigger lime juice
2 dashes grenadine
½ slice of pineapple

Mix drastically in an electric mixer, without ice.
Then pour onto shaved ice in a Mint Julep goblet or Collins glass, decorated with pineapple and slice of orange.

DR. COOK

Juice ½ lemon
White of 1 egg
Two dashes Maraschino
¾ gin (claret glass)

DU BARRY

⅔ English gin
⅓ dry vermouth
2 dashes Pernod
1 dash Angostura bitters

Stir well with ice and strain into glass. Serve with thin slice of orange.

DUBONNET

50-50 gin and Dubonnet. Stir with a citrus twist.

EARTHQUAKE

⅓ dry gin
⅓ whiskey
⅓ Pernod

Shake well with ice and strain into glass. It's been said by those who know that one of these should be sufficient.

ELEGANT

½ dry gin
½ dry vermouth
2 dashes Grand Marnier

Stir well with ice and serve.

EMERSON

Juice ½ lime
Small teaspoon Maraschino
⅓ Italian vermouth
⅓ Tom gin (stir)

FALLEN ANGEL

2 jiggers dry gin
Juice of 1 lemon or lime
2 dashes crème de menthe
1 dash Angostura bitters

Stir well with ice and strain into glass. Serve with cherry.

FARE-THEE-WELL

⅔ dry gin
⅓ dry vermouth
2 dashes sweet vermouth
6 dashes curaçao

Shake well with ice and strain into glass.

FIFTH AVENUE

½ dry gin
¼ sweet vermouth
¼ Fernet Branca

Stir well with ice and strain into glass.

FLORADORA

Juice ½ lime
½ teaspoon sugar
½ pony raspberry syrup
1 jigger gin

Frappé, fizz with ginger ale and serve in Tom Collins glass.

FREE SILVER

Juice ¼ lemon
⅓ spoon sugar
⅔ Tom gin
⅓ Jamaica rum
½ pony milk

Ice, shake and serve in tall glass, fill up with soda.

FRENCH 75

(Hotel Pfister, Milwaukee, Wisconsin)

Shake with cracked ice 1½ ounces dry gin, juice ½ lemon, ½ teaspoon powdered sugar. Pour into glass with ice cubes, fill with chilled champagne; add twist of lemon peel.

THE GIBSON

1 part French vermouth
5 parts gin

Stir gently in tall glass with ice, strain into cocktail glass, add cocktail onion, twist pieces of lemon peel over each glass, then drop peel into drink.

GIBSON GIRL

½ French vermouth
½ dry Tom gin (stir)

Squeeze lemon peel on top

A new one going the rounds is a "Ginsicle," a variation of Havana style Daiquiri. Fill a champagne glass with chipped ice, shaved fine. Pour over this half a jigger of fruit juice or prepared syrup, then add a jigger and a half of gin.

GILROY

⅓ dry gin
⅓ cherry brandy
⅙ dry vermouth
⅙ lemon juice
1 dash orange bitters

Stir well with ice and strain into glass.

GIMLET

3 parts dry gin
1 part lime juice

Shake with ice and strain into large 4-ounce cocktail glass. Add a dash of soda water.

GIN ALOHA

¼ ounce curaçao
1½ ounces gin
½ ounce unsweetened pineapple juice
3 dashes orange bitters

Shake, strain, garnish with maraschino cherry.

GIN BUCK

Place the juice of ½ lime and 2 twists of lime peel in a highball glass with 2 jiggers gin and ice cubes. Fill up with ginger ale.

GIN CUP

Take a pint cup, pure silver.
Fill it with crushed ice.
Put in juice ½ lemon.
Put in tablespoonful powdered sugar.
Joggle cup *slightly* for five minutes.
Add large jigger best gin.
Let stand until entire outside heavily frosted.

GIN JULEP

Bruise four sprigs of mint with a spoonful of powdered sugar. Add 2 ounces of gin. Fill tall glass with crushed ice and stir until frosted.

GIN ORANGUTAN

1 part simple syrup
2 parts lemon juice
Dash of orange bitters
8 parts gin

GIN RICKEY (Dry or Sloe)

Squeeze half a lime into ordinary bar glass, over cubes of ice. Toss in lime skin, add 1 jigger of gin and fill with soda water. Stir briefly. (Dash of grenadine sometimes added. For a sweeter drink, when dry gin is used, crush the lime-half with 1 teaspoon sugar before adding ice, gin, and soda.)

GIN AND SIN

¾ gin
⅛ orange juice
⅛ lemon juice
1 dash grenadine

Shake well with ice and strain into glass.

GIN SLING

3 jiggers of gin
½ jigger cherry brandy
½ jigger lemon juice
1 teaspoon of sugar
Piece of lemon peel and dash of bitters.

Pour into highball glass filled with ice. Add soda to fill.

Variation (1)

2 parts of gin
1 part of sweetened lime juice

Mix and pour into tall glass filled with shaved ice. Add soda water.

Variation (2)

2 jiggers of gin
½ teaspoon powdered sugar
1 teaspoon of sherry

Mix and pour into tall glass filled with ice.

Variation (3)

1 jigger of gin
1 spoonful lemon juice
1 spoonful sugar

Put fresh peach or strawberries in bottom of tall glass,

fill with ice and pour mixture in, adding soda water.

GIN SOUR

1 part sugar syrup
2 parts lemon or lime juice
8 parts gin

GIN SWIZZLE

1 ounce of gin
White of 1 egg
Juice of half a lime
Sugar to taste

Ice and shake and serve in tall glass.

Variation (1)

2 parts of gin
1 slice of lemon
1 spoonful of sugar

Shake and pour into tall glass filled with chipped ice, filling up with soda water.

Variation (2)

1/3 gin
1/3 brandy
1/3 French vermouth

Mix and pour into tall glass filled with chipped ice, fill up with soda water.

Variation (3)

1 jigger gin
1 teaspoon powdered sugar
2 dashes lemon juice
Slice of orange and pineapple

Pour into large glass filled with chipped ice.

Variation (4)

2 jiggers gin
2 dashes Cointreau
2 dashes French vermouth

Mix and pour into tall glass filled with ice, finish with ginger ale.

GIN & TONIC

(Mayflower Men's Bar, Washington, D. C.)

2 ice cubes in 8-ounce highball glass; squeeze 1/4 fresh lime, add rind for color, 1 1/2 ounces dry gin. Stir. Fill glass with tonic water and garnish with lime slice. Note: Don't stir after adding quinine water.

GOLDEN DAZE

2/3 jigger dry gin
1/2 jigger orange juice
1/3 jigger apricot brandy

Shake well with ice and strain into glass.

GREENBACK

1 part green crème de menthe
2 parts lime juice
8 parts gin

Strain lime juice to remove pulp and stir with large ice cubes.

GREEN DRAGON

1/2 dry gin
1/8 Kümmel
1/4 green crème de menthe
1/8 lemon juice

4 dashes peach bitters

Shake well with ice and strain into glass.

GREEN FIZZ

2 ounces gin
1 teaspoon sugar
1 teaspoon green crème de menthe
Juice 1 lemon
White of egg
Cracked ice

Shake well and serve.

GRENADINE COCKTAIL

1 teaspoon Framboise syrup
⅓ Oxygene Cusenier
⅓ gin
⅓ white mint

Shake well and strain into cocktail glass.

GRENADINE FIZZ

2 jiggers gin
2 teaspoons grenadine
Juice of ½ lemon

Shake well with ice and strain into glass. Fill up with soda water.

GYPSY

½ London gin
½ sweet vermouth

Stir well with ice and strain into glass. Serve with cherry.

HASTY

⅔ dry gin
⅓ dry vermouth
4 dashes grenadine
1 dash Pernod

Shake well with ice and strain into glass.

HEARST

1 dash orange bitters
1 dash Angostura bitters
½ jigger Italian vermouth
½ jigger gin

HOFFMAN HOUSE

2 dashes orange bitters
⅓ French vermouth
⅔ gin
Squeeze lemon peel on top

HOMESTEAD

⅔ dry gin
⅓ sweet vermouth
1 slice orange

Shake well with ice and strain into glass.

HONOLULU

⅓ Benedictine
⅓ gin
⅓ Maraschino

Shake. strain.

HULA-HULA

⅔ dry gin
⅓ orange juice
1 dash curaçao

Shake well with ice and strain into glass.

HURRICANE

⅓ dry gin
⅓ whiskey
⅓ crème de menthe
Juice of 2 lemons

Shake well with ice and strain into glass.

IMPERIAL

½ dry gin
½ dry vermouth
1 dash Angostura bitters
1 dash Maraschino

Stir well with ice and strain into glass. Serve with olive.

JAVA COOLER

3 hearty dashes Angostura bitters
Juice ½ lime
1½ ounces dry gin
Split of quinine water
2 cubes crystal-clear ice

Put the ice into a 10-ounce Collins glass. Squeeze in the juice of lime. Add bitters and gin. Fill glass with quinine water, stir slightly, serve with a stir rod.

JEWEL

⅓ dry gin
⅓ green Chartreuse
⅓ sweet vermouth
1 dash orange bitters

Shake well with ice and strain into glass. Serve with twist of lemon peel and, if you want, a cherry.

JOHN COLLINS

Follow directions for Tom Collins, below, but use Holland gin, pungently schnappy and a bit unexpected tasting at first sip.

JOURNALIST

⅔ dry gin
⅙ dry vermouth
⅙ sweet vermouth
2 dashes curaçao
2 dashes lemon juice
1 dash Angostura bitters

Stir well with ice and strain into glass.

KNOCKOUT

⅓ dry gin
⅓ dry vermouth
⅓ Pernod
1 teaspoon white crème de menthe

Stir well with ice and strain into glass. Serve with mint leaves.

LADY FINGER

½ dry gin
¼ Kirsch
¼ cherry brandy

Stir well with ice and strain into glass.

Lee Miller's FROBISHER

2 ounces gin
1 dash bitters
1 lemon peel
Plenty cracked ice

Combine in 10-ounce glass, then fill to brim with champagne. Stir.

LONDON

⅔ dry gin
2 dashes Maraschino
2 dashes sugar syrup
2 dashes orange bitters

Stir well with ice and strain into glass. Serve with twist of lemon peel.

LONDON BUCK

1 jigger dry gin
Juice of ½ lemon

Shake and serve over cracked ice in large cocktail glass, filling with ginger ale.

LOUD SPEAKER

⅜ dry gin
⅜ brandy
⅛ Cointreau
⅛ lemon juice

Stir well with ice and strain into glass.

MAIDEN'S PRAYER

(Served on the edge of the couch)

¼ dry gin
¼ Cointreau
¼ lemon juice
Dash of orange bitters

Ice and shake well.

MARGAES COCKTAIL

Jigger of supergrade gin escorting half-ounces each of lemon juice and pear juice; shooken, sieved, lemon-twisted.

MARGUERITE

⅔ gin
⅓ dry vermouth
1 dash orange bitters
1 twist orange peel

Stir well with ice and strain into glass. Serve with a cherry.

MARTINI

(Caucus Club, Detroit, Michigan)

Stir 2 ounces dry gin, 1 ounce dry vermouth with several ice cubes. Strain into frost-chilled cocktail glass. Twist skin-thin lemon rind over glass, to extract oil.

Note: Do not drop rind itself into glass.

DRY MARTINI (1)

1 part French vermouth
3 parts gin
Dash of orange bitters

Stir without great heat in tall glass half-filled with broken ice, then pour into cocktail glass. Twist a small segment of lemon peel (1 inch by ¼ inch) over the top then drop into glass.

DRY MARTINI (2)

1 part French vermouth
2 parts gin

Stir with ice in tall glass, until chilled. Serve in cocktail glass with green olive or pearl onion. Twist piece of lemon peel on top.

MEDIUM MARTINI

1 part French vermouth
1 part Italian vermouth
2 parts gin

Stir with ice in tall glass; strain into cocktail glass containing green olive.

SWEET MARTINI

Ladies Only

1 part Italian vermouth
1 part Tom gin
Dash of orange bitters

Stir with ice; serve with green

olive. Twist piece of lemon peel on top.

VARIATIONS: For spirited occasions a few drops of Pernod, Oxygene or the local absinthe adds just the right touch to the dry Martini. Sticklers insist that a small pickled onion be used in lieu of the olive when absinthe is used. Maraschino Benedictine, sprigs of mint, crème de menthe, orange peel and Angostura bitters are occasional "third rails" for the gin-vermouth combination.

MAURICE

½ dry gin
¼ sweet vermouth
¼ dry vermouth
Juice of ¼ orange
1 dash Angostura bitters

Stir well with ice and strain into glass.

MAXIM

1 ounce dry vermouth
1½ ounces dry gin
2 dashes crème de cacao

Shake, serve in pre-chilled cocktail glass.

MAYFAIR

½ dry gin
¼ apricot brandy
¼ orange juice
1 dash Pimento Dram

Shake well with ice and strain into glass.

MERRY WIDOWER

½ dry gin
½ dry vermouth
2 dashes Benedictine
1 dash Peychaud's bitters
2 dashes Pernod

Stir well with ice and strain into glass. Serve with twist of lemon peel.

MR. MANHATTAN

2 jiggers dry gin
4 dashes orange juice
1 dash lemon juice
4 crushed mint leaves
1 lump sugar moistened with water

Shake well with ice and strain into glass.

MONTREAL CLUB BOUNCER

1 part gin
1 part absinthe

Mix with cracked ice and, when frosted, sip slowly. (The legs are the first to go.)

MONTREAL GIN SOUR

1 part simple syrup
1 egg white
2 parts lemon juice
8 parts gin

Put all ingredients except the gin in shaker with cracked ice. Shake vigorously until thoroughly blended and creamy. Add about half the gin and combine, then add balance of gin and shake. Strain into chilled cocktail glass.

MOULIN ROUGE

½ orange gin
½ apricot brandy
3 dashes grenadine

Stir well with ice and strain into glass.

MOVE OVER

1 jigger gin
½ jigger French vermouth
¼ jigger Italian vermouth
2 dashes bitters
1 spoonful Cherry Heering

Shake lightly, strain, and add twist of lemon peel.

NEWBURY

½ dry gin
½ sweet vermouth
3 dashes curaçao
1 twist lemon peel
1 twist orange peel

Stir well with ice and strain into glass.

NIGHTMARE

⅓ dry gin
⅓ Dubonnet
⅙ cherry brandy
⅙ orange juice

Shake well with ice and strain into glass.

NINETEEN

⅓ dry gin
⅓ Kirsch
⅓ dry vermouth
4 dashes sugar syrup
1 dash bitters

Stir well with ice and strain into glass. Serve with cherry.

OPAL

½ dry gin
⅓ orange juice
⅙ Cointreau
¼ teaspoon powdered sugar

Shake well with ice and strain into glass. A little Orange Flower Water may be added, if available.

OPERA

⅓ gin
⅓ Dubonnet
⅓ crème de mandarine

ORANGE BLOOM

½ dry gin
¼ sweet vermouth
¼ Cointreau

Stir with ice and strain into glass. Serve with a cherry.

ORANGE BLOSSOM (1)

⅓ orange juice
⅓ Tom gin
⅓ Italian vermouth

ORANGE BLOSSOM (2)

2-3 jiggers dry gin
1 jigger orange juice

Stir well with cracked ice and strain into glass. Powdered sugar or sugar syrup may be added if desired.

PALE DEACON

3 jiggers grapefruit juice
2 jiggers dry gin
1 dash of powdered sugar

Shake with cracked ice, serve in frosted glass.

PALL MALL

⅓ English gin
⅓ dry vermouth
⅓ sweet vermouth
1 teaspoon white crème de menthe
1 dash orange bitters

Stir well with ice and strain.

PAPAYA SLING

5 dashes Angostura bitters
Juice of 1 lime
1 tablespoonful papaya syrup
1½ ounces dry gin

Put into 10-ounce highball glass. Add sufficient cracked ice. Fill with carbonated water, stir slightly.

PARADISE

⅓ apricot brandy
⅓ dry gin
⅓ orange juice
Dash of lime juice

Ice and shake well.

PARISIAN

⅓ dry gin
⅓ dry vermouth
⅓ Crème de Cassis

Stir well with ice and strain.

PARK AVENUE

1 part Italian vermouth
4 parts gin
2 parts pineapple juice
Dash of curaçao

Shake with cracked ice.

PENDENNIS COCKTAIL

¾ ounce Hungarian apricot brandy
1½ ounces gin
Add the juice of one lime or lemon
2 dashes of Peychaud bitters

Pour the mixture over cracked ice, strain into cocktail glasses.

PETER PAN

¼ dry gin
¼ dry vermouth
¼ orange juice
¼ peach brandy

Shake well with ice and strain into glass

PICCADILLY

⅔ dry gin
⅓ dry vermouth
1 dash Pernod
1 dash grenadine

Stir well with ice and strain into glass.

PING-PONG

½ sloe gin
½ Crème d'Yvette
Juice of ¼ lemon

Shake well with ice and strain into glass.

PINK LADY

¼ grenadine
¾ gin
White of 1 egg

Shake well with cracked ice. Strain into cocktail glass.

PLUIE d'OR

⅓ gin
⅓ Vielle Cure
⅙ curaçao
⅙ Kümmel

POET'S DREAM

⅓ Benedictine
⅓ French vermouth
⅓ gin

Lemon peel squeezed on top.

POLLYANNA

1 jigger dry gin
¼ jigger grenadine
¼ jigger sweet vermouth
3 slices orange
3 slices pineapple

Muddle the orange and pineapple slices in the bottom of a shaker. Add ice and the other ingredients. Shake well and strain into glass.

POLO (1)

⅓ dry gin
⅓ dry vermouth
⅓ sweet vermouth
Juice of ⅓ lime

Shake well with ice and strain into glass.

POLO (2)

⅔ English gin
⅙ grapefruit juice
⅙ orange juice

Shake well with ice and strain into glass.

PRAIRIE CHICKEN

1 pony of gin
1 egg in claret glass
Pepper and salt

Cover top with gin and serve.

PRINCETON

Dash of orange bitters
⅔ jigger Tom gin

Stir; fill with seltzer.

QUEEN BEE

⅔ sloe gin
⅓ curaçao
1 dash anisette

Shake well with ice and strain into glass.

QUEEN'S PEG

Pour ½ jigger dry gin over 1 ice cube in large wineglass. Then fill with iced champagne.

RACQUET CLUB

Dash of Orange bitters
½ gin
½ French vermouth
Orange peel

RAMOS, or NEW ORLEANS FIZZ

Juice of ½ lime and ½ lemon
1 ounce sweet cream
2 ounces dry gin
White of one egg
3 dashes Orange Flower Water

Shake with vim and vigor amid cracked ice. Pour into tallish glass, which has been dunked upside down in a saucer of lemon juice and then in powdered sugar, add seltzer stingily (or none at all) lest there be too much dilution. (*Note:* another recipe calls for ½ teaspoon powdered sugar. In any case, the secret is in long shaking. Twelve minutes is stated as the proper time.)

RAMOS GIN FIZZ

(Roosevelt Hotel, New Orleans, Louisiana)

In this order, fill cocktail shaker: 3 ice cubes, barspoon powdered sugar, 3 dashes Orange Flower Water, ⅓ ounce fresh lemon juice, ¼ ounce fresh lime juice, ½ ounce white of egg, 1¼ ounces gin, 2¼ ounces milk. Shake thoroughly. Strain into 7-ounce fizz glass.

RED LION

¾ ounce Grand Marnier
¾ ounce gin
Juice of ¼ lemon and ¼ orange

Shake, strain.

ROLLER DERBY

½ dry gin
¼ dry vermouth
¼ sweet vermouth
1 or 2 dashes Benedictine

Stir well with ice and strain into glass.

ROOSEVELT

½ Haitian rum
¼ French vermouth
⅛ orange juice
Dash of sugar syrup

Ice and shake well.

ROSE

¼ Grand Marnier
¾ gin

Ice, stir and serve.

ROSY DEACON

2 jiggers grapefruit juice
1 jigger sloe gin
1 jigger dry gin
1 dash powdered sugar

Shake with cracked ice, serve in frosted glass.

ROYAL FIZZ

1 jigger gin
1 egg
1 teaspoon sugar
Juice of ½ lemon

Shake well with ice and strain into glass. Fill up with soda water.

RUSSIAN

⅓ dry gin
⅓ vodka
⅓ crème de cacao

Stir well with ice and strain into glass.

SAN MARTIN

⅓ dry gin
⅓ dry vermouth
⅓ sweet vermouth
1 teaspoon anisette
1 drop bitters

Stir with cracked ice, strain into glass, first wetting the brim with lemon and sugar.

SAVANNAH

Juice of ½ orange
1 jigger of gin
White of egg
Dash of crème de cacao

SELF-STARTER

½ dry gin
⅜ Lillet
⅛ apricot brandy
2 dashes Pernod

Stir well with ice and strain into glass.

SEVENTH HEAVEN

½ dry gin
½ Dubonnet
2 dashes Maraschino
1 dash Angostura bitters

Stir well with ice and strain into glass. Squeeze orange peel on top. Serve with a cherry.

SHADY GROVE

2 jiggers dry gin
Juice of ½ lemon
1½ teaspoons sugar

Combine above ingredients in highball glass; add ice cubes, fill with ginger beer.

SILVER BULLET

½ dry gin
½ Kümmel
¼ lemon juice

Stir well with ice and strain into glass.

SILVER FIZZ

1 ounce lemon juice
1½ ounces exemplary gin
1 teaspoonful sugar
1 egg white

Shake furiously with cracked ice, strain into highball glass, fill up with sparkling water. Give stirring rod a couple of twirls in it.

SILVER STREAK

½ dry gin
½ Kümmel

Stir well with ice and strain into glass.

SINGAPORE SLING

1 jigger sloe gin
½ jigger dry gin
½ jigger apricot brandy
½ jigger cherry brandy
½ lime juice
1 teaspoon sugar

Serve in 12-ounce glass. Fill with ice and seltzer water. Decorate with cherry and slice of orange and pineapple.

SLEEPY HOLLOW

1 part simple syrup
1 part apricot brandy
4 parts lemon juice
10 parts gin
1 sprig mint

Muddle the mint with the lemon juice and sugar. Add the liquor and shake thoroughly over cracked ice.

SLOE GIN

Dash of orange bitters
⅔ sloe gin
⅓ Plymouth gin

Stir.

SLOE GIN FIZZ

1 jigger sloe gin
Juice ½ lemon
1 teaspoon powdered sugar

Shake well with ice, strain into highball glass and fill with soda.

SNYDER

2 dashes curaçao
⅔ dry gin
⅓ dry vermouth

Stir well with ice and strain into glass. Serve with ice cube and twist of orange peel.

Guy Lombardo's SOUPED-UP GIBSON

1 part vermouth
4 parts gin
6 pearl onions

SOUTH CAMP SPECIAL

(South Camp Road Hotel, Kingston, Jamaica)

¼ Jamaica rum
¼ dry gin
¼ Scotch
Dash of lime juice
Dash of sweet vermouth
Dash of cherry brandy

Shake well with cracked ice, strain into cocktail glass, and decorate with a cherry.

SOUTH SIDE

(Jack & Charlie's "21," New York City)

Briskly shake 1½ ounces gin and ½ ounce lemon juice with few leaves of fresh mint, sugar to taste, add ice cubes, then pour into a 4-ounce stemless glass. For added cooling appeal, sprinkle shredded mint bountifully.

SOUTHERN BRIDE

⅔ dry gin
⅓ grapefruit juice
3 dashes Maraschino

Shake well with ice and strain into glass.

SOUTHERN GIN

2 jiggers dry gin
2 dashes orange
2 dashes curaçao

Shake well with ice and strain into glass. Serve with a twist of lemon peel.

SPENCER

⅔ dry gin
⅓ apricot brandy
1 dash orange juice
1 dash Angostura bitters

Stir well with ice and strain into glass. Squeeze orange peel over top and serve with a cherry.

STAR DAISY

Juice ½ lemon
½ teaspoon powdered sugar
1 teaspoon grenadine
1 ounce dry gin
1 ounce applejack

Shake well with cracked ice and strain into stein. Add cube of ice and decorate with fruit.

SUBMARINE

½ dry gin
¼ Dubonnet
¼ dry vermouth
1 dash bitters

Stir well with ice and strain.

SUNSHINE

⅔ dry gin
⅓ sweet vermouth
1 dash Angostura bitters
1 lump of ice

Stir together and strain into glass. Squeeze orange peel over top.

SWAN

Juice of one lime
¼ jigger of gin
½ jigger of French vermouth
2 dashes Abbott's bitters
2 dashes of absinthe

TAHITI TYPHOON
(King-Size)

½ lime
1 ounce Cointreau
1 ounce gin
Split of chilled champagne

Squeeze lime in 14-ounce glass; add cracked ice and liquor; stir and fill with full split of champagne.

TANGO

½ dry gin
¼ sweet vermouth
¼ dry vermouth
2 dashes curaçao
Juice of ¼ orange

Stir well with ice and strain into glass.

TEX COLLINS

1 jigger gin
Juice ½ grapefruit
1 tablespoon honey

Stir well, add ice and fill tall glass with soda.

TEXAS RANGER

Juice ¼ grapefruit
1 teaspoon Maraschino
⅓ sweet vermouth
⅓ dry vermouth
⅓ dry gin

Shake well with ice, strain and serve with a few almonds.

TEXAS SPECIAL

2 parts gin
1 part cognac
1 part French vermouth
Dash of Cointreau
Juice of ½ grapefruit

Shake well with ice and serve.

THIRD DEGREE (1)

⅛ French vermouth
⅞ gin
Several dashes absinthe

THIRD DEGREE (2)

⅔ English gin
⅓ dry vermouth
4 dashes Pernod

Stir well with ice and strain into glass.

THREE STRIPES

⅔ dry gin
⅓ dry vermouth
3 slices orange

Shake well with ice and strain into glass.

TIDBIT

½ dry gin
½ vanilla ice cream
1 dash sherry

Shake well till thoroughly blended. If you think anything else is necessary, serve with a cherry.

TIPTOE

⅔ sloe gin
⅓ French vermouth
1 teaspoon lemon juice

TOM COLLINS (1)

(Racquet Club, Palm Springs, California)

Juice ½ lime, drop rind into 12-ounce glass with two ice cubes. Add ½ ounce fresh lemon juice, 1 spoon sugar, 1½ ounces gin, dash of Falernum. Fill glass with club soda. Add cherry.

TOM COLLINS (2)

Squeeze the juice of a lemon in a tall glass, add 1 heaping teaspoon of sugar, 1 generous jigger of Tom or London gin, plenty of cracked ice, and fill with soda water. It is well to stir before each gulp, as that keeps the sugar mixed and the drink effervescing. Variation: add several lusty shots of Angostura bitters.

TRILBY

Dash of orange bitters
⅓ French vermouth
⅔ Tom gin
1 dash of crème d'Yvette

TROPIC JINKS

1 generous jigger of gin
½ fresh lime
1 split of tonic water

Serve in regular highball glass with cube of ice.

TURF COCKTAIL

2 dashes orange bitters
2 dashes Maraschino
2 dashes absinthe
½ French vermouth
½ gin

Shake well, ice, and serve with olive.

TUXEDO

⅔ gin
⅓ gin
Dash of orange bitters

UNION JACK

⅔ dry gin
⅓ crème d'Yvette

Stir well with ice and strain into glass.

UNION LEAGUE

Dash of orange bitters
⅓ port wine
⅔ Tom gin

Stir.

VAN

⅔ dry gin
⅓ dry vermouth
2 dashes Grand Marnier

Stir well with ice and strain into glass.

VELVET HAMMER

1 ounce gin
1 ounce apricot brandy
1 ounce dry vermouth
1 dash Maraschino liqueur
1 dash orange bitters

Stir with ice, strain into standard cocktail glass; garnish with cherry.

VICTOR

¼ dry gin
¼ brandy
½ sweet vermouth

Stir well with ice and strain into glass.

VIRGIN

⅓ Forbidden Fruit
⅓ white crème de menthe
⅓ gin

Shake well and strain.

WAIKIKI BEACHCOMBER

¾ ounce gin
¾ ounce Cointreau
½ ounce fresh pineapple juice

Shake with cracked ice; strain into chilled cocktail glass.

WALLICK

½ dry gin
½ dry vermouth
3 dashes Orange Flower Water

Stir well with ice and strain into glass. Curaçao may be used in place of the Orange Flower Water.

WEDDING BELLS

⅙ cherry brandy
⅙ orange juice
⅓ gin
⅓ Dubonnet

WELCOME STRANGER

⅙ dry gin
⅙ Swedish Punch
⅙ Brandy
⅙ grenadine
⅙ lemon juice
⅙ orange juice

Shake well with ice and strain into glass.

WESTERN ROSE

½ dry gin
¼ dry vermouth
¼ apricot brandy
1 dash lemon juice

Stir well with ice and strain into glass.

WETBACK

3 dashes absinthe
1 part white crème de menthe
2 parts lime juice
8 parts gin

Strain lime juice, and stir with large ice cubes.

WHAT THE HELL

⅓ dry gin
⅓ dry vermouth
⅓ apricot brandy

4 dashes lemon juice

Stir well with ice and strain into glass.

WHITE ELEPHANT

⅓ Italian vermouth
⅔ dry gin
White of one egg

Judy Holliday's WHITE LADY

3 to 4 parts gin with 1 part Cointreau and 1 part fresh grapefruit juice. Pour the mixture into a Martini glass.

WHITE LADY (2)

1 part Triple Sec
2 parts lemon juice
8 parts gin
1 egg white

Put all ingredients except gin in shaker with cracked ice. Shake vigorously until thoroughly blended. Add half the gin and combine, then add balance of gin and shake. Strain into chilled glass.

WHITE LILY

⅓ dry gin
⅓ light rum
⅓ Cointreau
1 dash Pernod

Stir well with ice and strain into glass.

WHY NOT

⅓ dry gin
⅓ dry vermouth
⅓ apricot brandy
1 dash lemon juice

Shake well with ice and strain into glass.

WHITE PLUSH

2 jiggers dry gin
⅔ jigger Maraschino
1 cup milk

Shake well with ice and strain into glass.

WILL ROGERS

½ English gin
¼ dry vermouth
¼ orange juice
4 dashes curaçao

Shake well with ice and strain into glass.

YALE

Dash of orange bitters
½ Tom gin
½ Italian vermouth

Stir; add little seltzer on top.

YELLOW RATTLER

¼ dry gin
¼ dry vermouth
¼ sweet vermouth
¼ orange juice

Shake well with ice and strain into glass with small crushed pickled onion.

YOLANDA

¼ dry gin
¼ brandy
½ sweet vermouth
1 dash grenadine
1 dash Pernod

Stir well with ice and strain into glass.

ZAZA

2 dashes orange bitters
⅓ Tom gin
⅔ Dubonnet

Stir.

HOT DRINKS

ALE FLIP

Beat separately 2 egg whites and 4 yolks. Combine them, adding 4 tablespoons of moistened sugar, and ½ nutmeg grated. Put 1 quart ale in saucepan and bring to boil. Pour into it the egg-sugar mixture, gradually, stirring as you add.

Transfer the steaming result to robust pitcher and pour back and forth rapidly between this pitcher and its twin brother, each time holding the pourer high above the receiver, till a handsome froth is attained.

Serve in mugs or large goblets. One pillow to every customer.

Al Long's SPECIAL HOT TODDY

Juice of one lime
Sweeten 2 parts Drambuie, 1 part raspberry
2 ounces Scotch whisky
3 ounces boiling water

Mix and bring to boil.

APPLEJACK ALGONQUIN

1 teaspoonful baked apple
1 lump sugar
1 jigger applejack

Fill glass with hot water. Sprinkle with nutmeg.

ARCHBISHOP PUNCH

Stick cloves into a good-sized orange and roast it in a warm oven. When the skin is brown cut into quarters, seed, put into a saucepan and cover with a bottle of claret. Add sugar and let it simmer on fire until hot.

ARRACK PUNCH

Into a glass mug put:

1 ounce of orange juice
1 ounce of lemon juice
1 teaspoon sugar
1 jigger Arrack

Fill up with hot water. Stir. Give a ball of black tea a bath in it for two or three minutes, then remove. Add a slice of pineapple.

THE BEE-BEE

Dice the skins of citrus fruits, place them in the percolator where the coffee usually goes, pour honey over the dried fruit, then boil and percolate bourbon over them. This will bring on leprechauns and williwaws after the third, we guarantee.

BISHOP

Stick an orange full of cloves and roast it in front of the Yule log (or in the oven) until soft and brownish; cut it in quarters, pour over it a quart of hot port wine, and let simmer for half an hour. Serve in punch glasses. The aroma is almost as good as the flavor.

BLACK STRIPE (1)

(Served anywhere in the tropics)

1 tablespoon of honey dissolved in hot water
½ cocktail glass of old rum

Fill glass with hot water, grate nutmeg on top.

BLACK STRIPE (2)

1 wineglass rum
1 tablespoon molasses

Stir well in glass. Fill with hot water. Stir and serve with nutmeg on top.

BLUE BLAZER

1 jigger Scotch or rye
1 lump sugar
Very hot water
Set liquid on fire and pour from one glass to another
Twist of lemon peel on top

BOURGOGNE A L'ORANGE

(Serves 12)

2 bottles burgundy
Zest of 2 large oranges
Juice of half an orange
½ pint of boiling water
1 cup granulated sugar

Pare the zest from the orange very thin. Put in bowl and add sugar. Pour the ½ pint of boiling water over the sugar and zest and allow to infuse for 15 minutes. Add the juice of ½ an orange and the wine. Heat but do *not* boil. When very hot, serve with quarter-slice of orange stuck with clove.

BRANDY BLAZER

2 jiggers brandy
1 small twist orange peel
1 twist lemon peel
1 lump sugar

Place sugar in bottom of shaker and add other ingredients. Stir with a long spoon; blaze for a few second and extinguish. Strain into glass; to be served after dinner.

BRANDY PUNCH

Take the peel of two lemons, a pinch of cinnamon and a bit of nutmeg, mace and cloves Add this to three quarters-pound of sugar and a half-pint of boiling water. Let it simmer on the fire and then strain. Now add a bottle of brandy and the juice of two lemons. Added effect is gained by setting on fire before serving.

CAFE BRULOT

In a bowl put a glass of brandy. Then add two lumps of sugar, a half-dozen cloves, one stick of cinnamon, one piece of vanilla bean, a few pieces of dried orange and dried lemon peel. Stir these ingredients for a few moments, then add one pint of boiling coffee. Place a brandy-soaked lump of sugar in a spoon and ignite, then allow the flame to convey itself to the liquid in the bowl. Serve while still hot.

CAFE GROG

Mix 1 pony of Jamaica rum, 2 lumps of sugar, 1 slice of lemon, 1 spoonful of brandy and a demitasse of black coffee. Serve hot.

CAFE ROYALE

Place a lump of sugar in a spoon and balance over a demitasse cup of hot black coffee. Fill the spoon with brandy and when warm, blaze. As the flame begins to fade pour the contents into the coffee.

CHRISTMAS RUM PUNCH

6 oranges
½ gallon sweet rum
1 bottle Jamaica rum, bestest
Sugar to taste
Whole cloves
Ground cinnamon and nutmeg

Stick the oranges full of cloves and bake them in the oven until they soften. Place oranges in the punch bowl, pour over them the rum and granulated sugar to taste. Set fire to rum and in a few minutes add the cider slowly to extinguish the flame. Stir in cinnamon and nutmeg, and keep the mixture hot.

COLUMBIA

1 jigger rye whiskey
1 piece lemon peel
½ lump sugar

Fill with hot water.

EGGNOG
(For Solo Drinking)

Open fresh egg into large glass. Add two teaspoonfuls powdered sugar. Add small amount of milk and fill glass with very hot rum. Mix well and add dash Angostura bitters.

ENGLISH CHRISTMAS PUNCH

Take two bottles of good red wine, add one quart of strong tea, and the juice of one lemon and one orange. Heat thoroughly and just before serving, supporting on irons across the bowl two pounds of sugar soaked in rum. Light the rum and as the flame dies add the rest of the bottle of rum.

ENGLISH ROYAL PUNCH

1 pint hot green tea
1 pint hot cognac
½ pint dark rum
4 ounces curaçao
4 ounces Arrack
Juice of 2 limes
½ cup sugar
1 sliced lemon, peel and all

Thoroughly mix these ingredients, making sure that the sugar melts completely. Then add: whites of 4 eggs beaten stiff. Serve the English Royal hot but unboiled. This recipe should serve 10 people if served in average-size 5-ounce mugs, which by the way, should be preheated.

FLAMES OVER JERSEY

1 quart apple brandy
1 cup sugar
1 ounce to 1 jigger Angostura bitters
Lemon peels, to taste

Set afire and stir, with blue flames flickering (lights more easily if warmed first). Then douse flames with 1 quart boiling water, stir and serve pronto in glass or silver mugware.

GLOGG

Using a large pot, heat together 1 bottle port wine, 1 bottle of Burgundy wine, and 1 bottle aquavit with ¼ pound small seedless raisins, Boil several minutes. Into this dip cheesecloth bag containing stick of cinnamon and handful of cloves; leave bag in liquid about ½ minute. Serve drink in glass or coffee cup with almond in each glass.

GLOW WINE

2 bottles claret or other red wine
1 cup granulated sugar
6 cloves
Peel of ½ lemon
Piece of cinnamon

Bring to boiling point and serve at once with a slice of orange.

GOOD NIGHT ALL

1 gallon beer
½ pound honey
4 pinches pepper
4 pinches ground cloves
½ pinch ground ginger
2 sticks cinnamon

One day before serving, heat beer and honey together, stirring till latter is dissolved. Place spices in gauze bag and let steep in mixture.
Serve hot within easy access of bed. Germs of head cold, flu, etc. routed in one dose.

GLUEHWEIN

Boil in an earthen jug one glass of good claret or Burgundy. (Never use a fortified wine.) In the pot put about 3 inches of a cinnamon stick, 1 clove, 3 lumps of sugar, 1 slice of orange peel, and 1 slice of lemon peel. If a quantity is made it is better. Allow the earthen jug to stand on a slow fire and bring to near boiling point slowly.

GUARDSMAN'S PUNCH

(Serves 6)

1 ounce of port wine
1 pint of fresh green tea
4 ounces of sugar
Peel of one lemon
1 glass of brandy
1 bottle of Scotch whisky

Heat and serve piping hot.

Gus Goetz' APPLE DITLER

Quarter and core 4 eating apples. Boil in a half cup of water and one-half cup sugar to which add the grated rind and juice of half a lemon. When apples are tender remove to a plate, then add one cup of good white wine. Cook for ten minutes more and serve the apples with the hot sauce poured over the fruit.

HOT APPLE TODDY

¼ hot baked apple
2 teaspoons apple syrup
2 ounces apple brandy

Place all in very hot 10-ounce glass, fill with hot water, serve with nutmeg on top.

HOT BRANDY

1 teaspoon sugar, dissolved in boiling water.
1 wineglass brandy

Fill ⅔ with boiling water. Grate nutmeg on top.

HOT BRICK

Mix 1 teaspoon butter, 1 teaspoon sugar and 2 or 3 pinches of cinnamon in the bottom of a glass, adding 1 jigger of hot water to speed mixing. Add to this 1 jigger of bourbon. Fill the glass with steaming hot water. Serve and drink while still very hot.

HOT BUTTERED RUM (1)

(Olympic Hotel, Seattle, Washington)

Combine 1½ ounces gold rum, ¾ teaspoon brown sugar, 1 stick cinnamon, 1 clove, 1 pat butter in hot whiskey glass. Fill with boiling water, sprinkle with allspice.

HOT BUTTERED RUM (2)

(Bowl)

1 quart New England rum

3 quarts sweet cider
1 cup brown sugar
Enough butter to dapple the surface
1 cup boiling water

Dissolve sugar in 1 cup boiling water, add cider and heat to boil, then add rum, butter. Serve piping in punch bowl, flurried with ground cinnamon.

HOT BUTTERED TODDY

Bestow in deserving mug:

1 hooker doggonedest best whiskey
1 ounce orange juice
1 teaspoonful sugar

Fill up with hot water. Stir inhalingly. Add about a quarter of a pat of butter as a floater on top.

HOT GIN

2 jiggers gin
1 or 2 lumps of sugar
Juice of ½ lemon

Place in small tumbler and fill with hot water. Serve with a spoon.

HOT IRISH PUNCH (1)
(Individual)

Dissolve 2 lumps of sugar in a little hot water in large glass. Add small amount of lemon juice, and one wineglass Irish whiskey. Fill glass with hot water and stir well. Add nutmeg and slice of lemon.

HOT IRISH PUNCH (2)
(Bowl)

12 lumps sugar
2 lemons
1 bottle Irish whiskey
Cinnamon
Cloves
Boiling water

Rub sugar lumps on lemon rinds. Then squeeze lemons and muddle sugar in lemon juice. Add whiskey, cinnamon, cloves and boiling water to dilute as per own judgment.

HOT LOCOMOTIVE

1 egg yolk
½ tablespoon sugar
1 pony honey

Stir these well with a spoon. Add:

½ pony curaçao
1½ wineglasses Burgundy or claret

Place over fire until boiling. Pour from cooking dish to mug several times. Add slice lemon and little cinnamon.

HOT MINT BURGUNDY DELIGHT

6 fresh, crisp mint leaves
1 piece lemon peel
1 tablespoon sugar
3 ounces (or 3 tablespoons) Burgundy

Muddle well together and add a few drops of maraschino cherry juice syrup, one small stick of cinnamon and two whole cloves. Then add 3 ounces or 3 tablespoons of Burgundy and an equal amount of hot water. Stir and serve.

HOT MILK PUNCH (1)

1 tablespoon sugar
¼ wineglass rum
¾ wineglass brandy

Stir in large glass and fill with hot milk. Add nutmeg.

HOT MILK PUNCH (2)

Half wineglass of rum
Half wineglass brandy

Add spoonful powdered sugar. Mix well and pour into large glass. Fill glass with very hot milk. Add few grains nutmeg.

HOT MILK PUNCH (3)

1 teaspoon powdered sugar
1 pony curaçao
Dash of orange juice
Measure of rum

Mix in highball glass, fill with very hot milk and add a slice of orange and a few grains of nutmeg.

HOT RUM

Dissolve 2 lumps sugar in hot whiskey glass with a small amount of hot water.
1 wineglass dark rum
Juice of ½ lemon

Fill glass with hot water and sprinkle cinnamon on top.

HOT RUM PUNCH

1 pint Puerto Rico rum
½ pine cognac
½ wineglass Kümmel
½ wineglass Benedictine
1 lemon or lime peel
1 orange peel
1 sliced orange or grapefruit
1 sliced lemon or lime
Sugar to taste

Put all in bowl, add 3 pints boiling water. Stir well and serve.

HOT RYE

In a small tumbler dissolve 1 lump sugar in a very little hot water. Add 1 small piece cinnamon, 1 twist lemon peel and 2 jiggers rye whiskey. Serve hot water in a pitcher on the side, to be added as desired.

HOT SPICED WINE

Put a bottle of good American Burgundy or claret, without uncorking, into a deep pot of water atop a fire. Let it heat up, but don't let it actually boil, rescuing bottle when on the verge. Uncork and pour into preheated pitcher. Add hot syrup made with sugar and water, spiced as desired. Toss in sliced (or halved) lemons and oranges and any other flavorful cargo that occurs to you. Serve in glass mugs with a stick of cinnamon in each.

In instances where more intensive grape glow is required, a bottle of brandy is substituted for the wine, with 1½ quarts of water as dilutor. Where party opinion is stalemated on the question of Wine vs. Brandy, the solution is Hot Wine *with* Brandy—the brandy inserted to the extent of 3 ponies per bottle of wine; spices and décor same as in Hot Spiced Wine. The only hard and fast rule is: never let the wine or spirits boil.

HOT SPICED RUM

1 jigger dark rum
3 teaspoons sugar
2 teaspoons fresh butter
½ teaspoon mixed spices (powdered cloves, cinnamon)

Fill glass with boiling water. Stir well and serve.

HOT TEA PUNCH

(Serves 6)

1 pint Puerto Rico rum
1 pint brandy
2 sliced oranges
1 sliced lemon or lime
3 pints freshly brewed hot tea
Sugar to taste

And, oh yes, mull with red hot poker.

HOT TODDY (1)

(Individual)

Mix double shot of favorite whiskey or brandy with 1 teaspoon (or less) sugar. Fill glass with hot water and garnish with clove-studded lemon slice and bits of stick cinnamon.

HOT TODDY (2)

(Biltmore Hotel Men's Bar, New York City)

In 5-ounce glass mug, dissolve lump of sugar in few teaspoonfuls boiling water. Add 1½ ounces of your favorite whiskey. Fill mug with hot water, add twist of lemon peel and 5 cloves.

HOT TODDY (3)

(Bowl)

1 quart rye, bourbon, Scotch, apple brandy, or grape brandy
2 quarts boiling water
Clove-studded lemon slices
Bits of stick cinnamon
Sugar to taste

Pour boiling water over spiced and sugared liquor, stir, then serve steaming hot with one of the lemon slices in each drink.

HOT SCOTCH

1 or 2 lumps of sugar
Dissolve in hot whiskey glass with a little hot water
1 wineglass of Scotch whisky
Lemon peel

Fill glass with hot water, stir and add nutmeg.

HOT WINE PUNCH

Boil three spoonfuls of sugar in a half pint of water, add six cloves, three small pieces of stick cinnamon, rind of whole lemon cut very thin. When this comes to a boil, add one bottle of good claret or Burgundy and serve piping hot.

IRISH COFFEE

Into a prewarmed, stemmed glass pour a cup of very black, very hot coffee; add sugar to taste, a man-sized jigger of Irish whiskey, and top it all with a daub or a dollop of whipped cream, and you have a drink fit for an Irish king.

JAMAICAN HOT TEA PUNCH

1 pint voluptuous bodied bouquet rum
1 pint best brandy
2 oranges, sliced
1 lemon (or lime), sliced
3 pints hot tea, freshly brewed
Sugar to taste

Mix these in large metal pot on stove or in front of Yule fireplace. Mull by plunging in a red-hot poker as a stirrer. Makes six generous drinks, preferably served in jorums.

JERSEY MUG

Place in a heated mug 2 jiggers applejack, 1 good dash Angostura bitters, several whole cloves, and a large twist of lemon peel. Fill with boiling water and float applejack on top. Blaze and serve.

LAMB'S WOOL

(A corruption of "al maes abhal" ancient term for a harvest holiday, Nov. 1)

Put six baked apples in a large dish. Cut or break apples so that their pulp is exposed. Pour over these one quart of hot ale. Sugar to taste and add ginger and nutmeg in small quantities.

LIZARD SKIN

Hollow out half of a large orange. Pour in large jigger brandy. Light flame, extinguish after moment, and then drink.

MARCIA DELANO'S NORTHERN

1 tablespoon sugar
1 egg

Beat till stiff

½ glass Puerto Rico rum
¼ glass brandy

Fill glass with boiling water. Stir and serve with grated nutmeg on top.

MARQUISE PUNCH

1 pint cognac
1 quart sauterne
3 lemons
½ pound sugar
Cloves and stick cinnamon

Put wine, sugar, zest of lemons and spices together and heat slowly to a point where the wine starts to form.

MARTINIQUE MILK PUNCH

Bring a quart of grade A milk almost to the boiling point. Take from fire and add yolks of three eggs. Beat well, then add four tablespoons of sugar, and one quarter teaspoon of cinnamon, nutmeg and vanilla. Next add the peel of one lemon. Add one glass of rum and serve while still hot.

MULLED ALE

Heat an iron poker till red hot; immerse it slowly in a mug (preferably pewter) of ale, taking care not to cause an overflow.

MULLED CLARET

Into a large goblet or metal mug, place 1 lump of sugar, the juice of ½ lemon, 1 dash bitters, 5 ounces claret, 2 ounces of boiling water, 1 teaspoon of ground cinnamon, and stir. Heat a poker to a red-hot temperature and plunge it into mixture. Remove the poker and serve.

MULLED WINE (1)

1 pint Burgundy or claret, and extra glass of same
½ nutmeg
Sugar to taste
Yolks of 4 eggs

Grate nutmeg into pint of wine; sweeten to taste. Place on fire and bring to boil, then set aside for the moment.
Beat and strain the egg yolks, adding to them the glass of *cold* wine; then mix the result gradually with the *hot* spiced wine and pour back and forth half a dozen times.
Put total mixture on the fire and heat slowly till piping and thick. Ladle it up and down.
Serve in mugs with laths of toast on the side.

MULLED WINE (2)

(Mont Tremblant Lodge, Mont Tremblant, Quebec, Canada)

Heat 4 cups dry claret, slowly stirring in 2 sticks crushed cinnamon, 10 cloves, tablespoon sugar, 1 cup cognac, thin lemon peel. Bring *almost* to boiling point. Pour into warm pewter mugs. Dust with fresh nutmeg. Note: *never* allow boiling!

MULLED WINE WITH EGGS

Beat separately the whites and yolks of a dozen eggs. Pour two bottles of red wine into a saucepan thinning with half amount of water. Just before it comes to a boil, mix the whites and yolks together and stir them slowly into the hot wine. Serve from a pitcher with nutmeg grated on top.

NEGRITA GROG

¼ brandy
¼ rum
¼ sugar
¼ strong tea

Add a small glass curaçao, mix well, then pour into a large glass until it is half full. Fill the glass with hot water, slice of lemon on top.

NEGUS (1)

Pour a pint of port wine into a bowl and add ten lumps of sugar that have been rubbed on a lemon rind. Add the juice of one lemon. A small pinch of nutmeg. Now add a quart of boiling water and serve while hot.

NEGUS (2)
(Stronger)

Pare off yellow rind of one lemon in thin strips. Put into double boiler with juice of same, two tablespoons of sugar, and one bottle of port wine. Heat, stirring until sugar is dissolved. When hot, add one cup boiling water and strain into preheated pitcher. Pour into glasses or cups with or without a flick of nutmeg. Serves a dozen unless really thirsty.

NELSON'S BLOOD

½ glass of old rum
½ glass of hot water
1 lump butter

Put butter on top and as soon as melted: down the hatch.

NIGHT CAP

Beat up yolk of a fresh egg, add pony of anisette, one pony orange curaçao, one pony of brandy. Add hot water and leave a call for 2 o'clock.

OGGE

1 quart beer
2 ounces simple syrup
4 egg yolks

Beat syrup with yolks. Heat beer to boiling point, and stir gradually into yolk mixture. Dust with nutmeg.

OLD CASTLE PUNCH

Take a granite saucepan and melt two cups of loaf sugar in one quart of water, letting the mixture come to a boil. Now reduce the heat under the pan and add two bottles of Rhine wine, not permitting the mixture to boil. Soak a lump of sugar in a silver spoon. Pour gradually over the sugar a pint of good rum. Serve very hot as it comes off the fire.

PILGRIM HOT BUTTERED RUM

To brew the drink, one needs a copper or pewter pitcher, tall and stately in appearance —and it should be filled with cider brought to a boil, filling the room with a delicate fragrance.

Into a copper mug or pewter tankard, decant two ounces of Jamaica rum, one ounce of Calvados brandy of surprising vigor and undeniable mellowness. Next drop in a clove, a modest strip of lemon peel and a stick of cinnamon. Fill the mug nearly full with the boiling cider, swish it around with a spoon to assure proper blending, top with a pat of butter – and ceremoniously serve to the eager guest. (You can omit the rum and brandy, if you have guests who prefer it without the spirits, and still have a pleasant drink.)

REGENT'S PUNCH

Take two glasses of white wine and add one glass of Madeira and a half glass of rum. Mix this with one pint of very hot tea.

RUM AND BUTTER

1 cup of brown sugar
1 cup of boiling water
1 quart Jamaica rum
5 quarts of sweet cider
Butter

Put sugar and hot water in a large bowl. Dissolve sugar. Add the cider and heat to the boiling point–then add one quart of good Jamaica rum. Serve very hot with a little cinnamon, if desired, and enough butter to "film" the top of the liquid.

RUM FLIP
(For British Sailors)

1 egg
½ tablespoon powdered sugar
1 glass of rum, brandy, port wine, sherry or whiskey

Heat well, stirring constantly.

SACK POSSET
(A Two-Pot Circus)

Introduce to each other in a saucepan:

½ pint sherry (not "cooking" sherry)
½ pint ale

Slowly bring to a boil.
Meanwhile, in another saucepan, similarly heat up a quart of milk.
Pour the boiling milk gradually into the sherry and ale. Sweeten to taste. Add grated nutmeg.
Transfer to preheated dish or jug, equipped with a cover, and stand near fire for two or three hours. Quaff in mugs, preferably of the Toby type.

SANO GROG

Into a highball glass put a teaspoonful of powdered sugar, a pony of whiskey, a pony of curaçao, a pony of Jamaica or Bacardi rum. Add three times the quantity of boiling water. Serve with a slice of lemon on top.

SKI JUMPER'S THE DANSANT

1 pint strong hot green tea
Juice of 4 lemons and 6 oranges
½ pound granulated sugar, stirred till dissolved
1 wineglass curaçao or Triple Sec
1 bottle rum, heated

Serve hot and watch your slaloms.

SKIPPER'S PARTICULAR

1 pint Jamaica rum
½ pint cognac
2 ounces Kümmel
2 ounces Benedictine
Rind of 1 lemon
Ditto of 1 orange
3 pints of piping hot water
Sugar as you please

SOLDIER'S CAMPING PUNCH

1 large kettle boiled strong coffee
4 pounds lump sugar
4 bottles brandy
2 bottles Jamaica rum

Pour brandy and rum over sugar and place over fire until sugar is dissolved. Add to coffee mixture and stir well.

SUN VALLEY

Heat a quart of thick cream almost to the boiling point, add two tablespoons of powdered sugar. Beat the yolks of four fresh eggs with a little milk and add this to the cream. Now add a large glass of rum (Jamaica type) and stir thoroughly. Serve in cups.

THE AU KIRSCH

(Serves 20)

1 quart of Kirsch
1 quart of good black tea
12 tablespoonfuls of granulated sugar

Put the sugar in a hot bowl, pour over the Kirsch, heat a little and flame it for a few minutes. Put it out by slowly adding the quart of hot tea. A preserved cherry may be added to each glass, if desired.

THOMAS AND JEREMIAH

Into 1 big tall glass, pour 1½ jiggers of rum—white preferred. Add a touch of lime or lemon juice (preferably lime). Add brown sugar to taste. Fill with hot cider.

TOM AND JERRY (1)

(Version No. 999, geared for 12 portions)

Act I. Crack a dozen unquestionable eggs which have been chilled in the refrigerator; separate, beat the yolks thin and the whites thick, adding 3 tablespoons of sugar to the latter. Reunite actively, achieving a light batter.
Act II. Deal this out into mugs or tumblers—2 tablespoons apiece, plus 1 jigger of rye whiskey or brandy, and ½ jigger bouquet rum. Fill up with hot water or hot (not boiled) milk. Past masters employ an extra mug and pour back and forth from hand to hand—practically a triumphal arch in air. Nutmeg.

TOM AND JERRY (2)

Take as many eggs as persons served. Beat up the whites and yolks separately. Add one teaspoonful of granulated sugar for each egg and mix whites with yolks. When ready to serve, take two tablespoons of this batter and put in a large mug or tumbler. Now add one pony of brandy and one pony of Jamaica rum, stirring constantly to avoid curdling. Fill to the top with hot water or hot milk and stir until smooth. Usually a little grated nutmeg is sprinkled on top. (NOTE: Some, finding water too thin and milk too rich and filling, use half hot milk, half boiling water. Vary the proportions of rum and brandy, emphasizing one or the other, or try it with bourbon and brandy, bourbon alone or bourbon and rum.)

VIN CHAUD (Hot Wine)
(Skater's Delight)

Put 8 lumps of sugar, or 8 teaspoonfuls of granulated, into an earthenware bowl robust enough to stand flame under its belly. Pour in enough hot water to dissolve sugar.

Next, 1 bottle red wine, (Old-timers hold out for an able-bodied claret of, say, the St. Estephe or St. Emilion district, but will settle for Burgundy—jumping, in fact, if it's a *good* Burgundy.) Place bowl on the fire.

When smoking hot, but kept short of boiling, put in:

- 3 cinnamon sticks
- 8 cloves
- 4 slices of lemon
- Spiral-cut rind of 1 lemon à la sea serpent
- 3 prancing ponies of bouquet brandy

Keep on the fire so that it stays hot, but *never* let it boil.

WASSAIL BOWL (1)

Heat 1 quart of beer until it is warm, add 1 pound of sugar, a pinch of nutmeg, a pinch of ginger, a few slices of lemon peel. Then add four glasses of sherry and two more quarts of beer.

WASSAIL BOWL (2)

Put one pound of sugar in a bowl and over this pour three quarts of beer and four glasses of sherry. Add small amount of nutmeg and ginger and float a sliced lemon on top.

WHISKEY PUNCH

One pint of whiskey and two glasses of brandy are mixed with the juice and peel of one lemon. Then add one wineglass of boiling ale. Stir in one half pound of powdered sugar and a quart of boiling water.

ZERO NIGHT PUNCH
(Serves 6-8)

- ½ cup granulated sugar
- 1 quart milk
- 2 whole lemon peels, pared very thin

Place in double boiler, and let come to a boil. Infuse 5 or 6 tea bags for 1 or 1½ minutes. Remove bags and add 10 ounces apple brandy. Boil for 2 or 3 minutes, and serve very hot with a little nutmeg on the top.

BLACKTHORN

½ Irish whiskey
½ dry vermouth
3 dashes Pernod
3 dashes Angostura bitters

Stir well with ice and strain into glass.

BRAINSTORM

2 jiggers Irish whiskey
2 dashes dry vermouth
2 dashes Benedictine
1 twist orange peel

Place ingredients in Old-Fashioned glass with ice cubes.

EVERYBODY'S IRISH

1 jigger Irish whiskey
6 dashes green Chartreuse
3 dashes green crème de menthe

Stir well with ice and strain into glass. Serve with green olive.

IRISH

1 jigger Irish whiskey
2 dashes Pernod
2 dashes curaçao
1 dash Maraschino
1 dash Angostura bitters

Stir well with ice and strain. Squeeze orange peel on top.

IRISH COOLER

Place ice cubes in a large tumbler or highball glass with a long twist of lemon peel. Add 1 or 2 jiggers Irish whiskey and fill with soda water.

IRISH FIZZ

2 jiggers Irish whiskey
1 teaspoon curaçao
½ teaspoon sugar
Juice of ½ lemon

Shake well with ice and strain into glass. Fill up with soda water.

PADDY

½ Paddy's Irish whiskey
½ sweet vermouth
1 dash Angostura bitters

Stir well with ice and strain into glasses.

THE RED DEVIL

(Le Perigord Restaurant Sherry Netherland Hotel, New York City)

A potent concoction for that morning-after feeling. Also an excellent appetizer or apéritif: 2¼ ounces Irish whiskey, 1¾ ounces clam juice, 1¾ ounces tomato juice, few dashes of Worcestershire sauce, a pinch of ground pepper, and juice of ¼ lime. Shake (not too much) and strain into 6-ounce glass.

SERPENT'S TOOTH

2 parts Irish whiskey
4 parts sweet vermouth
2 parts lemon juice
1 part Kümmel
1 dash Angostura bitters

Stir well with ice and strain into glass.

SHAMROCK (1)

½ Irish whiskey
½ dry vermouth
3 dashes green Chartreuse
3 dashes green crème de menthe

Stir well with ice and strain into glass. Serve with green olive.

SHAMROCK (2)

Into a shaker, put 1 jigger Irish whiskey, ⅓ jigger dry vermouth, ⅓ jigger green crème de menthe. Shake well with ice. Strain into cocktail glass.

TIPPERARY

⅓ Irish whiskey
⅓ Chartreuse
⅓ sweet vermouth

Stir well with ice and strain into glass.

TOM MOORE

⅔ Irish whiskey
⅓ sweet vermouth
1 dash Angostura bitters

Stir well with ice and strain into glass.

PUNCHES

ADMIRAL RUSSELL'S PUNCH

Four hogsheads of brandy (a hogshead is 63 gallons), 250 gallons of Malaga wine, 20 gallons of lime juice, 2,500 lemons, 1,300 pounds of sugar, 5 pounds of grated nutmeg, and 8 hoghsead of water.

THE ALGONQUIN BAR PUNCH

½ barspoon of sugar
1 jigger sloe gin
¼ jigger Jamaica rum
1 jigger lemon juice
2 dashes raspberry syrup

Stir and pour into tall glass with cracked ice. Dress with fruit.

APPLEJACK PUNCH

(Serves 25-30)

2 quarts applejack
4 jiggers grenadine
1 pint orange juice

Combine the ingredients in a punch bowl with a block of ice. Just before serving add 2 quarts chilled ginger ale. Decorate with fruit if desired.

ARISTOCRAT SPARKLING PUNCH

1 bottle Burgundy
4 ounces brandy
1 quart sparkling water
2 bottles champagne
1 cup sugar

Dissolve sugar in a cup of sparkling water and pour into punch bowl. Add Burgundy and brandy, stirring well. Place block of ice in bowl, and add champagne and the balance of sparkling water. Garnish top of ice block with strawberries or raspberries, or other fruit in season, and float thin slices of two oranges on top of punch.

AULD MAN'S MILK

Half-pint Scotch
Quart cream
6 eggs beaten separately
1 teaspoon sugar

Sprinkle with nutmeg.

BALTIMORE EGGNOG

Take six eggs (fresh). Beat the yolks and whites separately. Beat until very light. Add ¼ pound of sugar to whites and ¼ pound of sugar to yolks. Beat again. Stir into the yolks one quart of rich milk and one quart of rich cream. Then stir in very slowly ¾ pint of Old New England rum, or Jamaica rum (a good heavy rum is best) and ¾ pint of good brandy. Whiskey may be used if desired, but real Maryland eggnog never has whiskey in it. Add ½ grated nutmeg and about two dozen whole cloves. Let stand in the refrigerator for about four hours before serving. When ready to serve, shake well to mix the milk and cream, which have a habit of separating.

ANOTHER BALTIMORE EGGNOG

One-fifth bottle cognac
1 pint Jamaica rum
½ pint apple brandy
½ pint peach brandy
2 dozen eggs
2 pounds powdered sugar
3½ quarts milk (or 3 quarts milk, one quart cream)
1 pint of thick cream

Beat the yolks of eggs until light, add liquors, starting with cognac, until the eggs are cooked. Next add sugar, beating it in, then the milk. Let stand in refrigerator or on cake of ice for 6 hours—or, if you're in a hurry, until cold. When ready to serve, fold in the whites stiffly beaten.

AND STILL ANOTHER
(This one with bourbon)

1 dozen fresh eggs
1 dozen tablespoons granulated sugar
1 pint best bourbon whiskey
1 pint heavy-bodied bouquet rum
1 wineglass peach cordial
1 quart milk
1 quart cream
Grated nutmeg

Segregate egg yolks, beat them and add them to the sugar, working it in gradually; then half of the milk. Still stirring, insert the whiskey and the rum. Let stand 15 minutes or so to give these elements a chance to get well acquainted; then add the other half of the milk, and also the cream, likewise the peach cordial. The whites of the eggs which have undergone a separate lashing till stiff, are now neatly folded into the mixture, which gets a light shower of nutmeg as a send-off.

BAYBERRY COVE PUNCH

Juice of 15 lemons
Juice of 4 oranges
1¼ pounds of powdered sugar
½ pint curaçao
1 glass grenadine
2 quarts of brandy
1-2 quarts sparkling water
Block of ice in punchbowl

BELLEVUE EGGNOG

One dozen eggs. Separate. Put whites aside for the moment. Beat yolks strenuously. While still beating, slowly add 12 tablespoons of granulated sugar and continue *a tempo* till sugar is entirely dissolved. Slowly pour in 1 generous pint cognac, still stirring the while. Follow with ½ pint (on the slim side) full-bodied rum. (The completed concoction should not taste of rum-in-the-nude. In other words, the rum must not boss the mixture. If it is very pungent, pull down the rum content and increase the cognac. In any case, the quality of the cognac will determine the character of the brew. So have your cognac good!) Pouring the liquor into the yolks has the effect of cooking them more lovingly than any stove could. Now take 1 pint milk and ½ pint heavy cream. (Cream may be whipped, but this makes the result a bit rich, so to some tastes plain cream is preferable.) Stir in milk and cream. Clean off egg-beating equipment and go at the whites till they will stand without hitching. Fold the whites into the general mixture. Then stir in 1 grated nutmeg. If outcome is too sweet to suit taste, extra brandy may now be added till it fits. Will serve 10 to 12 people. For openhouse purposes, you would need double, treble, or quadruple this amount. For convenience's sake, some people make this eggnog the day before the party and put it in the refrigerator till wanted. Parked there—or even on the pantry window sill—it will keep perfectly for several days if air-tight glass jars are used.

BOMBAY PUNCH

(Serves 35-40)

1 quart brandy
1 quart sherry
4 ounces Maraschino liqueur
½ pint Cointreau
4 quarts champagne
2 quarts sparkling water

Prechill all ingredients; pour into punch bowl embedded in cracked ice; add sliced fruits and halved, seeded grapes. Served in champagne glasses. Don't put ice in punch.

BOURGOGNE A L'ORANGE

(Serves 12)

2 bottles of Burgundy
Zest of two large oranges
Juice of half an orange
½ pint of boiling water
1 cup of granulated sugar

Pare the zest from the orange very thin—put it in a bowl and add the sugar. Pour the half-pint of boiling water over the sugar and zest and allow to infuse for fifteen minutes. Add the juice of half an orange and the wine. Heat but do *not* boil. When very hot, serve with quarter-slice of orange stuck with clove.

BOSTON FISH HOUSE PUNCH
(Serves 50)

Into the bosom of a mammoth punch bowl put:

1 tumbler melted sugar or plain syrup
1 tumbler lime juice (or 1½ tumblers lemon juice)

Mix thoroughly, making sure that all sugar is dissolved.
Now add:

1½ bottles superior Jamaica rum
1 bottle de luxe brandy
1 tumbler peach brandy
3 quarts champagne (cuvéed within our shores)
Hunks of ice

The impact of this punch is guaranteed to knock Santa Claus's beard right off its moorings, or break your lease if you so desire.

BRANDY PUNCH (1)

3 quarts of brandy
½ pint Jamaica rum
1 gallon water
Juice of six lemons
3 oranges sliced
1 pineapple pared and cut up
1 gill of curaçao
2 gills of raspberries
Falernum to taste
Ice

Mix the brandy, rum and curaçao—add the water, ice and Falernum, the lemon juice and fruit. Let it stand and serve very cold.

BRANDY PUNCH (2)

Juice 2 oranges
Juice 6 lemons
1 cup powdered sugar
½ pint curaçao
1 quart brandy
1 spoonful grenadine

Pour into punch bowl over a large piece of ice. Add 1 bottle soda water.

BUDDHA PUNCH
(Serves 10)

½ pint Rhine wine
4 jiggers orange juice
4 jiggers lemon juice
2 jiggers curaçao
2 jiggers medium rum
1 dash Angostura bitters

Combine in punch bowl with block of ice and just before serving add 1 bottle chilled soda water and 1 bottle chilled champagne. Garnish with twists of lemon peel and mint leaves.

BURGUNDY PUNCH
(Serves 24)

To 2 bottles of Burgundy, add 2 glasses of port, the juice of 4 oranges and 2 lemons, 2 slices of cucumber, sugar to taste, and plenty of ice. Finally add 2 quarts of mineral water.

CALIFORNIA EGGNOG
(Serves 12)

Take six fresh eggs and beat the yolks and the whites separately, particularly the yolks. Into the yolks, after having been beaten some time, beat

six tablespoons of sugar till smooth, six tablespoons of whiskey and one-half teaspoon of grated nutmeg. Then add the beaten whites. After adding the whites, add the following: six tablespoons brandy, three tablespoons rum.
When this is all beaten together, add one-half pint cream whipped stiff.

CHAMPAGNE CUP

Carve and shave a piece of ice 8 inches long so it will stand in a pitcher and leave 1½ inches space all around. In this space place 3 round slices of orange, 3 round slices of pineapple, and preserved cherries in between. 3 long slices of fresh cucumber rind are next put in place. Now add 1 bottle of champagne, and 2 ponies each of brandy and Benedictine, and stir. Fresh mint is used as top decoration.

Lily Pons' CHAMPAGNE FRUIT PUNCH

Marinate 12 hours in ice box 2 quarts Chablis, 2 diced pineapples. Pour into bowl. Add quart Chablis, simple syrup, lemon juice to taste, dash cognac, two bottles of champagne.

CHAMPAGNE PUNCH (1)

To each bottle of champagne add one bottle of club soda, one pony of brandy, one pony of Triple Sec liqueur; the rind of one orange, cut very thin. Little or no powdered sugar. And no lemon. Deposit berg of ice.
Decorate with sliced fresh pineapple and orange, and plenty of fresh mint. Crushed fresh strawberries add a gala touch to looks and flavor.

Variation

Cointreau instead of Triple Sec.

CHAMPAGNE PUNCH (2)

Mix well in a punch bowl that has been surrounded with cracked ice: ¼ pound powdered sugar, one glass brandy, one quart curaçao, one glass Maraschino, one quart sparkling mineral water, and two quarts champagne. Decorate with fruits in season. The addition of a spiral of cucumber rind gives this punch a unique and distinctive flavor.

CHAMPAGNE PUNCH (3)

(Recommended for summer; serves 10)

Slice four fresh pineapples, put them in your punch bowl and cover with sugar. Pour over this one pint of cognac and one pint of Jamaica rum, eight ounces of curaçao and the juice of six lemons. Put a cake of ice in the bowl and then slowly pour in four quarts of champagne. Decorate with slices of fruits.

CHAMPAGNE PUNCH (4)
(Serves 16)

Juice of 2 lemons
Juice of 1 orange
4 ounces brandy or rum
A little pineapple juice
1 bottle sauterne

Sweeten to taste, although this should be about right. Place in a punch bowl or pitcher with a large lump of ice and pour in a bottle of champagne.

CHAMPAGNE PUNCH (5)

Take 2 pounds of strawberries; cover with sugar, add a pint of champagne, let stand about five hours at room temperature. Then place a large cake of ice in the punch bowl and pour over it the strawberries and a 26-ounce bottle of cold champagne. Add 2 ounces of curaçao, let stand until the liquid becomes a delicate pink—then serve. The punch is deceptively smooth and charmingly sophisticated.

CHAMPAGNE SHERBET PUNCH
(Serves 18)

2 bottles champagne
1 bottle sauterne
1 quart of lemon or pineapple sherbet

Place sherbet in punch bowl. Pour iced champagne and sauterne around it. Be sure each glass has a serving of sherbet.

CHATHAM ARTILLERY PUNCH

1½ gal. Catawba wine
½ gal. rum
1 quart London dry gin
1 quart brandy
½ pint Benedictine
1½ quarts rye
1½ gals. strong tea
2½ lbs. brown sugar
Juice of 18 oranges
Juice of 18 lemons
1 bottle maraschino cherries

Mingle and let rest in a cold spot for 2 days. Then add 1 case champagne and serve. It's a drink you'll remember, if you remember anything.

CHRISTMAS RUM PUNCH
(Cold)

Juice of four oranges
Juice of two lemons
Diced pineapple
½ cup granulated sugar
1 pony curaçao
1 small bottle maraschino cherries
1 bottle old Jamaica or New England rum
1 bottle club soda

Place in punch bowl fruit juices, cherries and liquid of cherries; add garnishment consisting of 1 orange thinly sliced and 2 lemons ditto, and the diced pineapple. Also the sugar, curaçao and rum. Let stand for 2 hours. When due to be served add ice (chunk) and club soda.

CLARET OR BURGUNDY CUP

To each bottle of claret or Burgundy add one bottle of club soda, one glass of sherry, one pony of Triple Sec, and one pony of brandy; also the rind of one lemon cut very thin; powdered sugar to taste. Decorate with fresh pineapple, orange, and one slice of fresh cucumber rind. Let brew a short time before serving, then add a boulder of ice and, if available, a flock of fresh mint. Fresh (or frosted-packed) raspberries and peaches are appropriate dunnage.

COCKTAIL PUNCH

1 bottle sherry
1 bottle brandy
1 bottle sauterne

To a large punch bowl, add the sherry, brandy and sauterne, blending well by stirring. Add a large piece of ice. Stir until cold and add an equal amount of champagne just before you are ready to serve. This will make forty drinks.

COLD APPLE TODDY

Roast 1 dozen apples with their skins on. Mash while hot. Add 1 pound sugar and 2 quarts of boiling water. Then 1 quart apple brandy and 1 pint peach brandy. Cover so as not to squander aroma. And don't go sniffing at it.
When cool, strain coarsely, permitting pulp to come through. Add 1 pint sherry. Serve in bowl with ice.

CREAM IN YOUR COFFEE

3 quarts of hot coffee, turned loose upon:

1 quart vanilla ice cream
½ bottle Jamaica rum

Serve in bowl with ice. No décor.

EGGNOG NASHVILLE STYLE

The whites and yolks of eighteen eggs
1 quart bourbon (Bonded)
1 pint Jamaica rum
1 pint brandy
3 quarts heavy whipping cream
2 cups sugar, cloves, nutmeg

Christmas Eve

Mix the whiskey, brandy, rum, cloves and sugar. Allow to stand for six hours. Egg yolks, well-beaten, are added a little at a time. Cover bowl overnight.

Christmas Noon

Add stiffly beaten whites and cream separately, a little at a time. Drink. Freeze some for dessert at supper.

ELABORATE CUP

Take a large bowl and mix the following:

1 glass sherry
½ glass white curaçao
½ glass Maraschino

½ glass brandy
1 teaspoon bitters
1 slice cucumber peel
Rind of 1 lemon
3 slices orange
1 teaspoon simple syrup

Mix well, pour over large cake of ice, adding 1 bottle of champagne and 1 bottle of charged water. Serve in regular champagne glasses.

EMPIRE PUNCH

(Casino Bar, Dieppe)

In a large tumbler put three or four lumps of ice, then add:

1 teaspoon curaçao
1 teaspoon Benedictine
1 teaspoon brandy
1 wineglass of claret

Fill to top of glass with champagne, stir well, decorate with fruits.

ENGLISH ROYAL PUNCH

1 pint of hot green tea
1 pint of hot cognac
½ pint of dark rum
4 ounces of curaçao
4 ounces of Arrack
Juice of 2 limes
½ cup of sugar
1 sliced lemon, peel and all

Thoroughly mix these ingredients, making sure that the sugar melts completely. Then add: whites of four eggs beaten stiff.

Serve the English Royal hot but unboiled—a deep chafing dish with a low flame underneath is an ideal dispenser. This recipe makes about fifty ounces, or enough for ten people, when they're drinking out of average-size five-ounce silver, pewter, or ceramic mugs. (These, by the way, should be preheated with hot water.)

FESTOONERS' HIGH TEA

Rind of one lemon, cut thin
5 ounces lemon juice
2 quarts green tea, cold

Mix these well, then add:

1 bottle whiskey or brandy
4 ounces curaçao
1 bottle Angelica wine
1 bottle champagne or carbonated Moselle

Stir lightly and place in bowl containing berg of ice. Fruitage ad lib.

FLORIDA PUNCH

1 ounce grapefruit juice
1 ounce orange juice
1 ounce heavy rum
½ ounce brandy

Shake well and strain into tall glass filled with cracked ice.

FROZEN EGGNOG

(Algonquin Hotel, New York City)

(Serves 24)

12 egg yolks
1 pound sugar
1 gallon cream, whipped
1 pint brandy
1 pint Jamaica rum

Beat the egg yolks very light and add the sugar, then the whipped cream. Freeze till firm. Then add the brandy and rum and turn freezer rapidly a few times to mix well. Eat with holiday cake.

FRUIT CUP

Take whatever fruit you have on hand in season, such as peaches, strawberries, plums, raspberries. Wash the fruit, slice, put in a bowl with half a cup of sugar and one cup of brandy, rye or rum. Let it stand overnight and when ready to use pour into a gallon of chilled Chablis, Pouilly Fuisse or the best dry domestic white wine available. Variations: Use 1 cup sugar . . . add a quart of sparkling water and a glass of gin. The top of the bowl may be dressed with the fruits of the season.

GENERAL HARRISON'S EGGNOG

Use large tumbler. One egg; one and a half teaspoonfuls of sugar; two or three small lumps of ice. Fill the tumbler with cider and shake well.

GIN BOWL

1 gallon dry white wine (foreign or domestic)
1 bottle of gin
1 cup of green tea
3 lemons sliced

This can be stepped up considerably by the addition of one cup of heavy rum or brandy.

GOLDEN RETRIEVER PUNCH

1 pint lime juice
1 pint apricot syrup
3 pints orange
3 quarts club soda

Prepare mixture with exception of soda, which is to be added at time of serving, over large cake of ice.

GUARDSMAN'S PUNCH

1 ounce of port wine
1 pint of fresh green tea
4 ounces of sugar
Peel of one lemon
1 glass of brandy
1 bottle of Scotch whisky

Serve while hot.

HOLIDAY EGGNOG

Take six fresh eggs and beat the yolks and the whites separately. Add ½ cup of granulated sugar to the yolks, beating it in and add ¼ cup sugar to the whites after they have been beaten. Stir into the yolks one pint of rich cream and one pint of milk. Then stir in slowly one pint of good rye, bourbon or brandy and then one ounce of good heavy rum. Set aside for three or four hours so that the eggs will cook in the whiskey. When ready to serve, beat the whites in lightly and sprinkle nutmeg on top if desired. For serving, place in a container of ice.

IN THE GRAND MANNER

(Allow one fifth of champagne to each guest)

For every bottle of champagne add one pint of sparkling water, one wineglass of Maraschino, one wineglass of yellow Chartreuse and one full glass of the best cognac. Use one-half lemon and one orange, sliced, for each portion. Put a large chunk of ice in the bowl and serve cold.

JAMAICAN HOT TEA PUNCH

1 pint heavy-bodied bouquet rum
1 pint best brandy
2 oranges, sliced
1 lemon (or lime), sliced
3 pints hot tea freshly brewed.
Sugar to taste

Mix these in large metal pot on stove or in front of Yule fireplace. Mull by plunging in a red-hot poker as a stirrer. Makes six generous drinks, preferably served in jorums.

JEFF DAVIS PUNCH

1½ pints lemon juice
3¼ pounds sugar, dissolved in water
12 bottles claret
1½ bottles sherry
½ bottle brandy
½ pint Jamaica rum
1 cup Maraschino liqueur
3 bottles ginger ale
6 bottles mineral water or soda

Garnish with 2 lemons sliced thin; half of a cucumber sliced with peel on; one orange sliced.

If too strong, water may be added till the quantity reaches 5 gallons. Best if made 24 hours before using, adding ice, the ginger ale and mineral water just before serving.

JUBAL EARLY PUNCH

1½ gallons of lemonade
3 pints brandy
1 pint Jamaica rum
3 quarts champagne

Dissolve 1½ pounds of sugar in the lemonade before adding other ingredients. Bowl well iced.

KEUKA CUP

1 cup diced or crushed pineapple
1 orange, sliced
Juice of half a lemon
1 tablespoon grenadine
2 teaspoons sugar
1 bottle champagne

Commingle and chill, avoiding dilution by wilted ice. Serves 6-8 diffident people or 3 greedies.

LEONINE EGGNOG

12 eggs
12 level tablespoons granulated sugar
3 pints bouquet bourbon (rye if you prefer)
1 quart milk
1 pint heavy cream
Nutmeg

Crack eggs, separating yolks from whites. Setting latter aside for the nonce, go at yolks with an egg-beater, plying it furiously. Gradually add the sugar, beating it in till entirely dissolved. Now enters the whiskey, poured slowly and stirred, its action on yolks being equivalent to a gentle cooking. Then the milk, followed by the cream (whipped cream if you prefer extra richness), likewise stirred in. Clean off egg-beater and tackle the whites till they stand without flinching. Fold them into the general mixture. Stir in one grated nutmeg. Will serve 10 to 12 people. If it's the whipped cream version, they'll need spoons.

MARQUISE PUNCH

1 pint cognac
1 quart sauterne
3 lemons
½ pound sugar
Cloves and stick cinnamon

Put wine, sugar, zest of lemons and spices together and heat slowly to a point where the wine starts to form.

MEETING HOUSE PUNCH

(Serves 200)

4 barrels of beer
24 gallons of West Indies rum
35 gallons of New England rum
35 pounds of loaf sugar
25 pounds of brown sugar
465 lemons

MILK PUNCH

1 teaspoon of sugar
2 pieces of ice
½ cocktail glass of rum (or brandy or whiskey)

Put in shaker and fill with rich milk. Shake well and serve with nutmeg on top.

MINT JULEP, Community Style

Take your punch bowl and place it on a table under a tree. Next fill it half full of chipped or shaved ice. Now in a separate crock place about fifty fresh mint sprigs. Pour over these a glass of water, a glass full of rum, one-fourth pound of powdered sugar and then macerate the leaves thoroughly. When infused, pour this through a cocktail strainer, over the chipped ice. Do not permit any of the stems or mash to seep through. Next pour on two bottles of best bourbon. Now place straws around the edge of the bowl, the sort that will last a few moments. Use as many straws as you have guests. At a given signal, tell them to heave to.

MISSISSIPPI PUNCH

Stir in Collins glass:

2 dashes lemon juice
1 teaspoon sugar
2 dashes Angostura bitters

Add:

1 ounce whiskey
1½ ounces rum
1 ounce brandy

Fill with cracked ice; garnish with fruit if desired; attack with straws.

MYRTLE BANK PUNCH

Combine in shaker with a large piece of ice 1 jigger Demerara Rum (151 proof), juice of ½ lime, 6 dashes grenadine and 1 teaspoon sugar. Shake and pour over cracked ice in a 10-ounce glass. Float Maraschino liqueur on top.

NOEL ON THE NOSE

Assemble and boil together for five minutes:

½ cup sugar
¾ cup water
6 strips lemon peel
12 cloves
3-inch stick of cinnamon

Let cool and strain. Now add:

1 cup orange juice
½ cup lemon juice
1 cup juice of canned pears
1 bottle American red wine
1½ cups sparkling water

Pour over ice hunk in the punch bowl. Garnish with orange and lemon slices and cut-up canned pears.

OLD CASTLE PUNCH

Take a granite saucepan and melt two cups of loaf sugar in one quart of water, letting the mixture come to a boil. Now reduce the heat under the pan and add two bottles of Rhine wine, not permitting the mixture to boil. Soak a lump of sugar in a silver spoon. Pour gradually over the sugar a pint of good rum. Serve very hot as it comes off the fire.

OLD VIRGINIA EGGNOG
(Thick)

12 eggs, new born
2¼ cups granulated sugar
1 quart finest brandy
1 pint Jamaica rum, rich and ripe
1 gallon heavy cream

Beat the 12 yolks relentlessly, adding the granulated sugar, then alternate shots of the brandy and rum till full amounts are incorporated. Then three-fourths of the heavy cream and, foldingly, half of the egg whites, pre-beaten in a side dish. Whereupon, beat up other half of egg whites stiffer than stiff, adding to them the cup of powdered sugar, plus (lightly stirred in) the other quart of cream, and fold this latter into the former. Set aside for twelve hours in a cool place. Serve with spoons.

OLD WALDORF CHAMPAGNE PUNCH

Put ice in a punch bowl and add one small glass brandy, one liqueur glass maraschino, one liqueur glass Benedictine.

one barspoon pulverized sugar, one quart champagne, and one pint aerated water. Use plenty of fruit in season, and mix well.

ORANGE CUP

(Serves 12)

Juice of sixe oranges
2 pints carbonated water

Sweeten with sugar and put in punch bowl with:

16 ounces of rum
2 ounces curaçao
Iceberg

PICNIC PUNCH

(Ideal for washtub and cake of ice)

(Serves 30)

1 pineapple, cut up
12 lemons, cut up
1 gallons gin
2 gallons white wine
1 pint of rum

PINEAPPLE PUNCH

(Serves 10)

1½ quarts Moselle wine
Juice of 3 lemons
5 dashes Angostura bitters
2½ jiggers English gin
⅔ jigger pine syrup
⅔ jigger grenadine
⅔ jigger Maraschino

Pour all together into punch bowl with 1 quart chilled soda water. Set bowl in bed of crushed ice to chill. Decorate with pineapple.

QUICK PUNCH

One of the best champagne punches is easily made and can be rushed in for an emergency. Slice some large oranges in a bowl, add a chunk of ice and pour champagne over this, in quantities according to the number of guests.

RAPPAHANNOCK EGGNOG

1 dozen egg yolks (no whites used at all)
12 even tablespoons pulverized sugar
3 pints bouquet bourbon whiskey
3 wineglasses peach brandy
2 wineglasses full-bodied rum with plenty of "nose" to it
3 pints milk
1 pint whipped cream

Beat yolks in a kitchen bowl for 30 minutes. (An electric mixer is a good reprieve.) Add the sugar gradually, with no letup; then, shot by shot, the 3 liquors, followed by the milk. Last of all, the whipped cream is inserted after a 12-hour rest.

RED WINE CUP

1 bottle of claret or Burgundy
1 bottle of club soda
1 wineglass of sherry
1 pony curaçao
1 pony brandy
Rind of 1 lemon, cut very thin

Smidgen of powdered sugar

Adorn with fresh pineapple, orange, fresh mint and slice of fresh cucumber rind. Let stand an hour. Add large berg of ice when ready to serve.

REGENCY PUNCH

Take two glasses of white wine and add one glass of Madeira and a half-glass of rum. Mix this with one pint of very hot tea.

REGENT PUNCH

(One gallon)

1 pint black or green tea, brewed strong
Thin-cut rinds of 4 lemons
1½ pounds granulated sugar
Juice of 6 lemons and 6 oranges
1 pint brandy
1 pint rum
1 magnum (or 2 bottles) champagne

Put the lemon rinds into the tea while the latter is still hot, allowing them to seep together. Add the sugar. Set aside to cool.

When cold, add the lemon and orange juices, the brandy and the rum. Place in punch bowl with one or two large chunks of ice, adding the champagne immediately before serving. Garnish with orange and pineapple slices.

RHEIMS PUNCH

(Serves 12)

Combine ½ cup of sugar, three sliced oranges, juice of five lemons, six slices of pineapple (cut in small pieces), maraschino cherries. Pour over this three quarts of chilled champagne, and add one quart orange sherbet which dissolves and cools the punch.

RHINE WINE PUNCH

(25-30 cups)

3 quarts Rhine wine
1 quart chilled soda water
2½ jiggers brandy
2½ jiggers Maraschino
1 cup strong tea
½ pound powdered sugar

Combine all the ingredients in a punch bowl set in a bed of crushed ice. Decorate with fruit as desired and serve when thoroughly chilled.

ROUND ROBIN DIP

1 gallon dry white wine
1 bottle of gin
1 cup of green tea
3 lemons sliced

This can be stepped up by the addition of one cup of heavy rum or brandy.

ROYAL MILK PUNCH

1 glass milk
1 tablespoon sugar
1 egg
1 jigger rum

Shake with cracked ice, strain into highball glass and serve with grated nutmeg on top.

RUBY PUNCH

(Serves 18)

Juice of 2 lemons and 2 oranges
1 wineglass brandy
1 wineglass curaçao
1 wineglass raspberry syrup
2 bottles sparkling Burgundy
1 quart sparkling mineral water

Mix all ingredients except the sparkling Burgundy and sparkling water in a punch bowl with ice. Add Burgundy and water last, stirring lightly.

RUM PUNCH (1)

Into a bowl put ½ cup granulated sugar and juice of 4 large grapefruits. Stir to dissolve the sugar and add 1 bottle of rum, 4 ounces brandy and 4 ounces of Benedictine, 2 teaspoons of bitters, and the juice of 1 lime. Stir well and add ½ nutmeg grated and the peeling of 1 lime.

RUM PUNCH (2)

Pour over fine ice in tall glass:

2 ounces rum
Juice of ½ lime
1 teaspoon sugar

Stir; stick in some mint sprigs and that does it. No shaking. No decorating. Just drinking.

SAUTERNE PUNCH

Slice some peaches and apricots (twice as many of the former), add 4 ounces brandy, cover with sugar and let stand for a few hours. When ready to serve, put the mixture in a bowl or pitcher and pour over it one bottle chilled sauterne and one split charged water. Ice slightly so as not to weaken the drink.

SCHUYLKILL PUNCH

(Serves 50)

Slack ¾ pound of loaf sugar in punch bowl. When dissolved, add:

1 quart lemon juice
2 quarts of Jamaica rum
1 quart cognac
2 quarts water
1 wineglass peach brandy

Put in punch bowl with large cake of ice and allow to brew for two hours before serving.

SCOTCH PUNCH

2 quarts of Scotch whisky
1 pint of good brandy
1 cup of green tea
Rind of 6 lemons
1 teaspoon of cloves
1 tablespoon of allspice
30 lumps of sugar

Seal this in a glass jug and allow to stand at least *six* weeks before serving. Served with ice, either cracked in the glass, or a chunk in the punch bowl will modify the single potion.

SHERRY EGGNOG

Use large bar glass. One fresh egg, ½ tablespoon of sugar. Fill the glass with fine ice, then 1 pony of brandy and 1 wineglass of sherry. Shake well and strain into thin glass, sprinkle nutmeg on top.

SHERRY WINE PUNCH

Pour into large bar glass ½ wineglass Orgeat syrup, 1 or 2 dashes of lemon juice. Fill glass with shaved ice. Then pour in 1½ wineglasses of sherry while stirring. Dress with fresh fruit and float on a little claret.

Sinclair Lewis's ARROWSMITH PUNCH

⅓ pint lime or lemon juice
¾ pound of sugar dissolved in water
½ pint cognac
½ pint peach brandy
¼ pint Jamaica rum
2½ pints carbonated water

Add large piece of ice and serve from punch bowl.

SIR CHARLES PUNCH
(Christmas)

Fill a large tumbler half-full with shaved ice. Add to this 1 teaspoon granulated sugar, 1 wineglass port, ½ glass of brandy, ½ glass curaçao. Stir well with a spoon. Ornament the top with slices of orange, pineapple and split grapes.

SOLDIERS' CAMPING PUNCH

1 large kettle boiled strong coffee
4 pounds lump sugar
4 bottles brandy
2 bottles Jamaica rum

Pour brandy and rum over sugar and place over fire until sugar is dissolved. Add to coffee mixture and stir well.

STRAWBERRY BOWLE

Place in a bowl one quart of washed and hulled strawberries. (Use wild strawberries, if possible.) Cover with 1 cup sugar and 1 cup cognac. Shake bowl slightly to mix ingredients and put in icebox to stand about eight hours. When ready to serve, add three bottles of well-iced Moselle or Rhine wine. Do not add ice.

TEA PUNCH

Use a pint of strong tea, a pint of sherry and a half-pint of Jamaica rum. Add the juice of maraschino cherries (a small bottle). When cold, add bits of orange and lemon peel before serving.

THE AU KIRSCH
(Serves 20)

1 quart of Kirsch
1 quart of good black tea
12 level tablespoonfuls of granulated sugar

Put the sugar in a hot bowl—pour over it the Kirsch—heat a little and flame it for a few moments. Put it out by slowly adding the quart of hot tea. A preserved cherry may be added to each glass, if desired.

WHISKEY PUNCH

Add the juice and peel of one lemon to one pint of whiskey and two glasses of brandy. Then boil a half pint of ale stirring into half a pound of powdered sugar and about a quart of boiling water. Add this to the other mixture and serve.

WHITE WINE CUP

1 bottle of white Burgundy or dryish Graves
1 bottle of club soda
1 wineglass of sherry
A pony apiece of anisette and brandy
Rind of 1 lemon
Powdered sugar in moderation
Thin slices of fresh pineapple
Mint
Ice

WORLD OF TOMORROW PUNCH

Use an extra large bowl. 1½ pounds of loaf sugar are rubbed on the yellow skins of 4 fine lemons and 2 oranges until the colored parts of the fruit have been rubbed into the sugar. Place in the bowl slices of 1 pineapple, 1 dozen fine oranges, sliced, 1 box of strawberries, 2 bottles of the best sparkling water, and mix these ingredients thoroughly. Now add ⅛ pint of Maraschino, ⅛ pint of curaçao, ⅛ pint of Benedictine, ⅛ pint of rum, 1 bottle of brandy, 6 bottles of champagne, 4 bottles of Tokay wine, 2 bottles Mareira, 4 bottles fine claret, and mix well with ladle. Strain through a very fine sieve into a clean bowl surrounded with ice. Serve in wineglass.

WRIGHT SPECIAL

6 jiggers of rye
6 jiggers of port wine
Juice of 3 lemons
4 teaspoons of sugar

Shake in a shaker with cracked ice, then add the beaten whites of 3 eggs.

YANKEE PUNCH

2 quarts rye whiskey
1 pint New England rum
6 lemons, sliced
1 pineapple, sliced
4 quarts of water
Sugar to taste
Ice

ZERO NIGHT PUNCH

(Serves 6-8)

½ cup granulated sugar
1 quart milk
2 whole lemon peels, pared very thin

Place in double boiler, and let come to a boil. Infuse 5 or 6 tea bags for 1 or 1½ minutes. Remove bags and add 10 ounces apple brandy. Boil for 2 or 3 minutes, and serve very hot with a little nutmeg on the top.

RUM

AIR MAIL

Mix in shaker:

Juice of one-half lime
1 teaspoon honey
1 jigger gold rum

Add cracked ice, shake; strain into highball glass and fill with dry champagne.

BACARDI COCKTAIL

1. *The pink kind:*

Juice of 1 lime
½ teaspoon sugar
1½ ounces Bacardi rum
Dash of grenadine

Shake well with fine ice; strain into cocktail glass.

2. *Variations on the theme:*

Juice of half a lime
1 teaspoonful of grenadine
1 part gin
2 parts Bacardi

BACARDI COLLINS

Mix in shaker:

Juice of one lime
1 teaspoon sugar
1 jigger Bacardi

Shake well with ice; strain into Collins glass ballasted with ice cubes. Fill with soda water.

BACARDI FIZZ

2 jiggers Bacardi rum
1 teaspoon sugar
Juice of ½ lemon

Shake well with ice and strain into glass. Fill with soda water.

BAKER'S DOZEN

Prepare and slice four large pineapples. Let them soak for an hour or longer in the following: one pint of Jamaica rum, one pint of brandy, four ounces of curaçao, the juice of six lemons and one pound of granulated sugar. When ready to serve place cake of ice in center of the bowl and then pour in six bottles of champagne.

BATISTE

⅔ rum
⅓ Marnier

BEACHCOMBER

1 jigger Maraschino
1 jigger lemon juice
4 jiggers rum

BEE'S KISS

1 jigger rum
1 teaspoon honey
1 teaspoon cream

Shake well with ice and strain into glass.

BLACK ROSE

In a tumbler or highball glass, with 2 cubes of ice, place 1 teaspoon sugar, 1 jigger rum and fill with cold black coffee. Stir and serve.

BLACK STRIPE

1 wineglass rum
1 tablespoon molasses

Stir well in glass. Fill with hot water. Stir and serve with a little nutmeg on top.

BOLERO

1 ounce simple syrup
8 ounces dark rum
3 ounces lime juice
8 ounces cognac
1 teaspoonful orange juice for each glassful

Shake with finely crushed ice and strain into cocktail glass.

BOLO

2 jiggers light rum
Juice of ½ lemon or lime
Juice of ¼ orange
1 teaspoon powdered sugar

Shake well with ice and strain into glass.

BOMBO

2 ounces rum
2 ounces water
1 stick of long sugar (sugar cane)

BROADMOOR COOLER

(Broadmoor Hotel, Colorado Springs, Colorado)

In a 14-ounce shell glass 1½ ounces light rum, a dash of green crème de menthe, ½ lime and juice; fill with Seven-Up. Glass edge should be rubbed with mint. Top with sprig of mint.

BROWN DERBY

4 ounces dark rum
1 teaspoon maple sugar
Juice of one lime

Shake well and serve.

BUCK JONES

Put jigger of rum in highball glass
1 jigger of sherry
Juice of ½ lime

Fill with ice and dry ginger ale.

BUSHRANGER

½ light rum
½ Dubonnet
2 dashes Angostura bitters

Shake well with ice and strain into glass.

THE BYRD

Fry six rashers of fat bacon. When done add one pint of good rum. Eat the bacon and drink the syrup.

CAFE GROG

Mix a pony of Jamaica or Bacardi rum, two lumps of sugar, a slice of lemon, a spoonful of brandy and a demitasse of black coffee. Serve hot.

CAPTAIN'S BLOOD

1 ounce lime juice
4 ounces Jamaica rum
2 dashes Angostura bitters

Shake with finely cracked ice.

CARIBBEAN CAPER

Bore out one of the eyes of a coconut and drain off the milk. Mix half milk and half Jamaica rum, ice, and fill with charged water.

CARIBE WELCOME

(Caribe Hilton, San Juan, Puerto Rico)

To 1 ounce of light rum and 1 ounce apricot liqueur, add 1 ounce coconut cream and 3 ounces coconut water. Mix thoroughly and pour into coconut shell. Fill to brim with crushed ice.

CHARLEY COLLINS

1 tablespoon fresh lime juice
½ tablespoon of sugar
1 jigger rum
2 lumps of ice

Put in highball glass and fill with charged water.

CHINESE

⅔ Jamaica rum
⅓ grenadine
3 dashes curaçao
3 dashes Maraschino
1 dash Angostura bitters

Stir well with ice and strain into glass. Serve with cherry.

COLUMBIA COLLINS

(Columbia Restaurant, Tampa, Florida)

Combine 1 jigger light rum, 2 ounces fresh grapefruit juice, dash fresh lemon juice, 1 teaspoon brown sugar. Decorate with fresh mint, slice of orange and lemon.

CHRISTOPHE

⅓ gin
⅔ Haitian rum
Dash of sugar
Peel of a lime

Ice and shake well.

COMMODORE PERRY

½ teaspoon sugar
1 dash lemon juice
White of one egg
1 jigger rum
1 dash of grenadine
1 dash of raspberry syrup

COOL O' THE EVENING

Crush thoroughly 1 sprig mint in shaker. Add juice ¼ lemon, ½ teaspoon sugar, 1 jigger white rum, cracked ice. Shake till heavy frost. Strain into cocktail stemmer. (You may substitute *white* créme de menthe for mint.)

COOW-WOOW

½ glass of rum
½ glass of water
1 large punch ginger

CRYSTAL RUM FIZZ

1 jigger Haitian rum
2 jiggers ginger ale
1 Cryst-O-Mint Life Saver

(The Life Saver is used to take the curse off the rum. It should not be allowed to dissolve, but should be stirred gently and used again for the second, third, and fourth drinks. After that, you won't miss it.)

CUBA LIBRE

Juice of half a lime (or lemon)
2 ounces Puerto Rican rum with cracked ice in highball glass

Fill with Coca-Cola.

DAIQUIRI COCKTAIL (1)

Juice of half a lime
1 jigger (1½ ounces) white rum
1 barspoon powdered sugar

Shake vimfully with cracked ice till shaker frosts; strain into cocktail glass.

Variations on the theme: Some insist they form a more perfect union by adding a dash of white Maraschino liqueur; others interpolate a squirt of Triple Sec. Still others pink the whole situation up with grenadine, in which case we are out of the Daiquiri category entirely but by no means in the bleak wilderness if bright eyes have anything to say about it.

DAIQUIRI (2)

(George Washington Hotel)

Mull lump of sugar in juice of one lime
Add generous jigger Cuban rum

Shake and serve in glass filled with fine ice.

DAIQUIRI DELUXE

1 ounce Orgeat or Crème d'Ananas
3 ounces citrus juice (mixed lemon and lime)
16 ounces Cuban rum

Shake vigorously with plenty of finely crushed ice and strain into chilled and frosted cocktail glass.

DAIQUIRI GRENADINE

1 ounce simple syrup
3 ounces lime juice
16 ounces light rum
2 dashes grenadine

Stir sugar, grenadine, and lime juice together thoroughly before adding the rum.

DAVIS

½ Jamaica rum
½ dry vermouth
2 dashes raspberry syrup
Juice of 1 lime

Shake well with ice and strain into glass.

DESSALINES

½ Haitian rum
¼ Clairin
¼ whiskey
¼ lime juice, dash of sugar

Ice and shake well.

EL PRESIDENTE

Over ice in a tall mixing glass, pour:

1 ounce white Cuban rum
½ ounce orange curaçao
½ ounce dry vermouth
Dash of grenadine

Shake or stir well, then strain into cocktail glass. (When stirred instead of shaken, it will pour a delightfully clear, deep orange color.) A twist of orange peel may be added.

EYE-OPENER

Liqueur glass old Haitian rum
Teaspoon grenadine
Yolk of one egg
2 dashes of curaçao
2 dashes of apricot brandy

Ice and shake well.

FLANAGAN

1 jigger Jamaica rum
1 jigger sweet vermouth
½ teaspoon sugar syrup
1 dash Angostura bitters

Shake well with ice and strain into glass.

FLORIDA PUNCH

1 ounce grapefruit juice
1 ounce orange juice
1 ounce heavy rum
½ ounce brandy

Shake and strain into tall glass filled with cracked ice.

FLORIDITA SPECIAL

(Serves 4)

Put into your blender glass:

4 ounces rum
2 level teaspoons granulated sugar
2 teaspoons grapefruit juice
2 teaspoons Maraschino liqueur
Juice of one medium lime
Three cups of finely cracked ice

It is extremely important not to alter the order of ingredients. Chill your cocktail glasses by pouring in cracked ice and a little water. Now you're ready to freeze-spin your Daiquiri. Hold on the top of the blender and turn to *high speed.* Blend ingredients for about twenty seconds. This will require careful watching. This Daiquiri, when perfect, should be the consistency of lightly frozen sherbet.

FOG CUTTER

1⅓ jiggers Puerto Rican rum
⅔ jigger brandy
⅓ jigger gin
⅔ jigger orange juice
1 jigger lemon juice
⅓ jigger Orgeat syrup
Sherry

Shake all the ingredients, except the sherry, with cracked ice and pour into a 14-ounce glass with the ice. Float the sherry on top and serve with straws.

FOR VISITING AUNTS

Brew tea to proper strength, put in pitcher and ice. Add rum until it tastes right, decorate with cut fruit, or better, slices of lemon and a sprig of mint. Delicious at luncheons.

FOX TROT

2 jiggers light rum
2 dashes curaçao
Juice of ½ lime or lemon

Shake well with ice and strain into glass.

FLYING TIGRE COCTEL

½ gold rum
¼ gin (or more)
¼ grenadine (or less)
Bitters
Sugar

Shake with fine ice. Then pour without straining into large cocktail glass.

HAITIAN COCKTAIL

1 jigger Haitian rum
1 jigger fresh lime juice
1 spoon powdered sugar

Ice, shake and serve in cocktail glass.

HAITIAN RUM PUNCH

3 parts of Haitian rum
1 part of sugar
Peel of lime
Dash of bitters

Ice and stir a little.

HARPO'S SPECIAL

2 ounces rum
1 drop bitters
½ teaspoon curaçao
Juice of one-half lemon
½ teaspoon sugar

Shake well and strain.

HONEY BEE

1 part honey
4 parts Bacardi
1 part lemon juice

Mix well, then add ice and shake.

HONEYSUCKLE

1 part honey
2 parts lemon juice
8 parts Cuban rum

HOP TOAD COCKTAIL

Juice of ½ lime
1 part Puerto Rican dark rum
1 part apricot brandy

HOTEL DRAKE VESUVIUS

Juice ½ lemon
1 teaspoon sugar
1 jigger orange juice
¾ jigger gold rum
¾ jigger Jamaica rum
4 dashes red fruit coloring

Shake well and strain into nine-ounce highball glass filled with shaved ice. Decorate with fruit and sprig of mint. Place the glass so that it rests on a cake of dry ice at bottom of a sixteen-ounce glass. In space between glasses pour hot water over dry ice. Use of dry ice gives a smoky effect.

I DIED GAME

1 jigger Haitian rum
1 jigger apricot brandy
1 splash of drinking water

(Most sincere drinkers do not care for this one as they say the water adds an unfamiliar tang that they can't learn to like.)

JAMAICA GINGER

⅔ Jamaica rum
⅓ grenadine
3 dashes Maraschino
3 dashes curaçao
1 dash Angostura bitters

Shake well with ice and strain into glass.

Bob Crosby's KAILUA COCKTAIL

1½ jiggers Puerto Rican dark rum
1 jigger pineapple juice
⅓ jigger lemon juice
⅓ jigger of grenadine

Serve in punch cups.

Douglas Edwards' ZOOMAR COCKTAIL

Shake jigger dark Puerto Rican rum, jigger pineapple juice, dash grenadine, dash lime, shaved ice. Serve in chilled glass

KINGSTON (1)

½ Jamaica rum
¼ Kümmel
¼ orange juice
1 dash Pimento Dram

Shake well with ice and strain into glass.

KINGSTON (2)

1 jigger Jamaica rum
½ jigger gin
Juice of ½ lime or lemon
1 teaspoon grenadine

Shake well with ice and strain into glass.

Oliver La Farge's LAUGHING BOY COCKTAIL

Dissolve half a teaspoon of sugar in a dash of Angostura

bitters. Add 1 teaspoonful of sweet vermouth. Add chipped ice. Fill Old-Fashioned glass to brim with New England rum. Garnish with lemon peel and slices of orange (if you like fruit salad).

LITTLE PRINCESS

½ light rum
½ sweet vermouth

Stir well with ice and strain into glass.

THE LUCIE

(Chez Lucie, New York City)

⅓ Grand Marnier
⅓ rum
½ juice of lime
Dash of orange curaçao

Serve in champagne glasses. Trim glasses with sugar.

MIAMI

1 jigger light rum
½ jigger white crème de menthe
2 or 3 dashes lemon

Shake well with ice and strain into glass.

MISSISSIPPI PUNCH

Stir in Collins glass:

2 dashes lemon juice
1 teaspoon sugar
2 dashes Angostura bitters

Add:

1 ounce whiskey
1½ ounces rum
1 ounce brandy

Fill with cracked ice; garnish with fruit if desired; attack with straws.

MT. BAKER BEAKER

Juice of half a lemon, heaping teaspoon sugar, or to taste, well dissolved; 2 ounces dark rum; 50–50 mixture of canned pineapple juice and water, to fill up the highball glass. Serve well iced; or hot, with a little melted butter.

NAKED LADY

½ light rum
½ sweet vermouth
4 dashes apricot brandy
2 dashes grenadine
4 dashes lemon juice

Shake well with ice and strain into glass.

NATIONAL

1⅓ jiggers light rum
⅓ jigger pineapple juice
⅓ jigger apricot brandy

Shake well with shaved ice and strain into glass. Serve with pineapple (stick or wedge) and cherry.

NAVY GROG

(Don, The Beachcomber, Chicago, Illinois)

Mix over cracked ice: ¾ ounce each fresh lime and grapefruit juice, simple syrup; 1 ounce each Demerara rum, Jamaica rum, Puerto Rican rum, club soda. Form ice-cone mold around straw in 14-ounce grog glass and add mixture.

NELSON'S BLOOD

½ glass of old rum
½ glass of hot water
1 lump of butter

Put butter on top and as soon as melted let the drink slide down the hatch.

NEVADA

1½ jiggers light rum
Juice of ½ grapefruit
Juice of 1 lime
1 dash Angostura bitters
1 teaspoon powdered sugar

Shake well with ice and strain into glass.

NUGENT

2 ounces rum
1 teaspoon sugar
½ white of egg
Juice of ½ lemon

Shake well with ice and strain.

OLYMPIA

1 jigger dark rum
⅔ jigger cherry brandy
Juice of ½ lime

Shake well with ice and strain into glass.

PALMETTO COCKTAIL

1 ounce Jamacia rum
1 ounce Italian vermouth
Dash of orange bitters

PANAMA

1 jigger Jamaica rum
½ jigger crème de cacao
½ jigger cream

Shake well with ice and strain into glass.

PARADISE

1½ jiggers light rum
½ jigger apricot brandy

Shake well with ice and strain into glass.

PAULINE

½ rum
½ sweetened lemon juice
1 dash Pernod
1 grating of nutmeg

Shake well with ice and strain into glass.

PEG O' MY HEART

½ lime juice
½ Cuban rum
Color with grenadine

PENNSYLVANIA

1 ounce grenadine
3 ounces pineapple juice
16 ounces light rum

Shake with cracked ice.

PETION

⅓ rum
⅓ Benedictine
⅓ Clairin
Lime juice and sugar

Ice and shake well.

PILGRIM

1 jigger New England rum
1 teaspoon grenadine
Juice of ½ lime or lemon

Shake well with ice and strain into glass.

PIRATE'S

3 ounces dark rum
1 sweet vermouth
1 dash Angostura bitters

Stir well with ice and strain into glass.

PLANTER'S PUNCH (1)

(As made and served in Jamaica for residents)

1 ounce fresh lime juice
2 teaspoons sugar, mix together, then add:
4 ounces old Jamaica rum
2 ounces water and ice

Shake and serve very cold.

PLANTER'S PUNCH (2)

(As served for American tourists)

1 teaspoon sugar
2 ounces fresh lime juice
3 ounces water and ice
4 ounces old Jamaica rum

Fill glass with cracked ice, then add half-slice of lemon, orange, pineapple, and cherry. Put sprig of mint on top.

Patrice Munsel's PLANTER'S PUNCH

1 ounce lime juice
1 teaspoon brown sugar
3 ounces dark Jamaican rum
3 ounces water

Stir sugar, water in pitcher. Add juice, ice and rum. Stir. Serve in tumblers or cocktail glasses.

PLANTER'S PUNCH (3)

(Boca Raton Club, Boca Raton, Florida)

Shake with cracked ice, juice ½ lemon, juice ½ orange, juice ½ lime, 1½ ounces light rum, 2 dashes pineapple juice, 2 dashes grenadine and 1 teaspoon powdered sugar. Strain into chilled glass. Add ice cube. Decorate with fruit and mint.

PLATINUM BLONDE COCKTAIL

1 ounce rum
1 ounce Cointreau
½ ounce sweet cream

Shake with cracked ice; strain into chilled cocktail glass.

POLO COCKTAIL

One ounce lemon juice
One ounce orange juice
Two ounces Puerto Rican dark rum

PRESIDENTE VINCENT

½ rum
¼ French vermouth
Lime juice and sugar

Ice and shake well.

PRINCE GEORGE

⅓ Grand Marnier
⅔ rum
Juice of ½ lime
Twist of lemon peel

ROBSON

½ Jamaica rum
¼ grenadine
⅛ orange juice
⅛ lemon juice

Shake well with ice and strain into glass.

ROOSEVELT

½ Haitian rum
¼ French vermouth
⅛ orange juice
Dash of sugar syrup

Ice and shake well.

ROYAL BERMUDA

2 ounces Barbados rum
Juice 1 lime
Little sugar syrup
1 dash Cointreau

Shake with shaved ice and strain into glass.

ROYAL MILK PUNCH

1 glass of milk
1 tablespoon of sugar
1 egg
1 jigger of rum

Shake with cracked ice, strain into highball glass and serve with grated nutmeg on top.

ROYAL RESERVE

Put one lump of ice in tall glass.

1 jigger of rum

Fill up with dry ginger ale.

THE RUBY

1 jigger of rum
Juice of 1 orange
4 dashes of blackberry brandy
1 teaspoon powdered sugar

Shake thoroughly with chipped ice until glass is frosted, garnish with fruit and a sprig of mint and serve with straw.

RUM COLLINS

Juice of 1 lime or one half lemon
1 teaspoon sugar
2 ounces rum

Shake with ice, pour unstrained into Collins glass and fill with sparkling water. Or mix juice and sugar in bottom of glass, add ice cubes, then pour in rum and seltzer. Bottled Collins mix can be used: ice cubes, then rum, then bottled mix.

De luxe version

Use 1 tablespoon Falernum in place of sugar. Variation: add a dash of Angostura bitters.

RUM DUBONNET

½ jigger rum
½ jigger Dubonnet
Juice of one half lime

RUM FIZZ

1 jigger of rum
1 dessert spoon of sugar
1 egg

Shake well with chipped ice and pour into tall glass. Fill to top with soda water.

RUM FRAPPE

Place 1 scoop orange or lemon sherbet in a champagne glass and cover with rum as desired. Stir and serve.

RUM ORANGE COCKTAIL

¼ orange juice
¼ Italian vermouth
½ rum
1 pinch powdered cinnamon

Ice, shake well, and serve in cocktail glass.

RUM PUNCH

Pour over fine ice in tall glass:
1½-2 ounces your favorite rum
Juice of half or whole lime
1 teaspoon or more sugar syrup, to taste

Stir, stick in some mint sprigs and the show is complete. No shaking. No fruiting. Just drinking.

RUM SCAFFA

Place in a cocktail glass 1 dash Angostura bitters and ½ each Benedictine and rum.

RUM SIDECAR

Equal parts rum, lemon juice, Triple Sec

RUM SOUR (1)

¾ ounce lemon juice
¼ teaspoon sugar
1¼ golden lightbodied rum

Shake with ice; give glass a "lid" of 151 proof rum.

RUM SOUR (2)

1 teaspoon plain syrup
Juice of one half lime
Half-cocktail glass of rum

Ice and shake and pour into small glass. Decorate with fruit if wanted and/or with a few drops of egg white.

RUM SWIZZLE

3 parts rum
1 part Falernum
Juice of ½ lime
2 dashes Angostura

Shake vimfully; strain into Delmonico glass. Note: If you *must* be authentic in your swizzling, you'll frost with a plantation-grown swizzle stick (plural-forked twig, peeled) rotated between your palms so that it zizzes in the finely crushed ice.

RUNT'S AMBITION

2 ounces rum
2 ounces gin
2 ounces whiskey
2 ounces port wine

Shake with ice; strain.

SANTA CRUZ RUM DAISY

Fill a goblet ⅓ full of shaved ice and add 3 dashes sugar

syrup, 3 dashes maraschino or curaçao, juice of ½ lemon and fill with rum.

SANTIAGO

1 part curaçao
2 parts lime juice
8 parts light rum
2 or 3 dashes Jamaica rum

Shake with cracked or crushed ice.

SAXON

1 jigger rum
2 dashes grenadine
1 twist orange peel
Juice of ½ lime

Shake well with ice and strain into glass.

SEPTEMBER MORN

Juice of one lime
One jigger rum
White of one egg
Color with grenadine

Serve in claret glasses.

SHANGHAI

1 jigger Jamaica rum
⅔ ounce lemon juice
⅓ ounce anisette
2 dashes grenadine

Stir well with ice and strain into glass.

SHAUN BANIGAN

1 ounce Puerto Rican light rum
1 ounce Jamaica rum
1 teaspoonful of sugar
1 teaspoon lemon juice
Dash of bitters

SKI JUMPER'S THE DANSANT

1 pint strong hot green tea
Juice of 4 lemons and 6 oranges
½ pound granulated sugar, stirred till dissolved
1 wineglass curaçao or Triple Sec
1 bottle rum, heated

Serve hot and watch your slaloms.

SKIPPER'S PARTICULAR

1 pint Jamaica rum
½ pint cognac
2 ounces Kümmel
2 ounces Benedictine
Hide of 1 lemon
Ditto of 1 orange
3 pints of piping hot water
Sugar as you please

SONORA

½ light rum
½ Calvados or applejack
2 dashes apricot brandy
1 dash lemon juice

Stir well with ice and strain into glass.

STERLING

1 jigger orange juice
2 jiggers rum
½ jigger Benedictine

Shake until the glass is frosted, garnish with fruit, serve with straws.

SUBURBAN

Dash of orange bitters
Dash of bitters
1/5 port wine
1/5 Jamaica rum
3/5 whiskey

SUICIDE COCKTAIL

1 ounce of Haitian rum
1/2 ounce crème de cacao
1 ounce soda water
1 Cryst-O-Mint Life Saver dropped from a great height

(In preparing this drink, the glass is placed on the floor and the mixer stands erect, holding the Life Saver at shoulder height. If he misses the glass three times in a row, he does not need another drink—not very badly, anyway.)

SUNSHADE COCKTAIL

Equal parts pineapple juice, dry vermouth, white rum. Dash of grenadine. Stir with cracked ice.

TOWER ISLE COCKTAIL

3/4 ounce rum
1/2 ounce crème de cacao
1/2 ounce cocoanut cream

Shake well in ice, serve in Martini glass with a cherry. Repeat, smiling broadly.

Gypsy Rose Lee's VAN VLEET COCKTAIL

3 jiggers light rum
1 jigger maple syrup
1 jigger lemon juice

Shake well with cracked ice and serve like a Daiquiri. Pre-chill glass.

WHAT'S IT?

White of one egg
1/2 jigger Jamaican rum
1/2 jigger port wine

Ice, shake, serve in eight-ounce glass, fill up with soda.

Alexander Woollcott's WHILE ROME BURNS COCKTAIL

1 part lemon juice
2 parts Medford rum
1 dash of maple syrup

ZOMBIE A LA PUERTO RICO

Onto cracked ice in shaker pour:

3/4 ounce pineapple juice (unsweetened)
3/4 ounce papaya nectar (canned)
Juice of sizable lime
3/4 barspoon powdered sugar
1/3 ounce apricot brandy
1 ounce Puerto Rican, white, 86 proof
2 ounces Puerto Rican, gold, 86 proof
1 ounce Jamaican heavy-bodied, 90 proof

Shake. Without straining, pour into Zombie glass, adding cubed ice to nearly fill. Bedoll with sprig of mint, small square of pineapple; skewer 2 cherries on toothpick and set so that it bridges the rim. Carefully pour on a shallow float of tropical heavy-bodied 151 proof, Sprinkle a light flurry of powdered sugar. Pair of straws.

ZOMBIE A LA NO. I BOY

Juice of one lime
1 barspoon brown sugar
1 barspoon passion fruit
3/4 ounce Puerto Rican or Cuban, white
3/4 ounce Puerto Rican or Cuban, gold
3/4 ounce 90-proof Jamaica
1 ounce 151-proof Demerara

Stir together all these ingredients except the last; pour into 14-ounce glass which has been filled three-fourths full of cracked ice; float the 151-proofer as a lid; garnish with mint or fruit. A straw proposition.

ZOMBIE (3)

2/3 jigger Jamaica rum, 90 proof
1 1/3 jiggers dark rum, 86 proof
2/3 jigger light rum, 86 proof
2/3 jigger pineapple juice
2/3 jigger papaya juice, if available
Juice of 1 lime
1 teaspoon powdered sugar

Shake well with ice and pour into 14-ounce glass. Decorate with pineapple and cherry and float on top Demerara rum, 151 proof. Sprinkle lightly with powdered sugar and serve.

RYE AND BOURBON

Note: Use rye and/or bourbon when specified; use blended whiskeys when recipe is not specific.

Benny Goodman's ADMIRAL COCKTAIL

1 ounce bourbon, 2 ounces dry vermouth and juice of ½ lemon. Shake well with ice cubes. Pour. Lemon twist.

AFTER-DINNER SPECIAL

(Ciro's, Hollywood, California)

In a pony (liqueur) glass put equal portions: ⅓ Benedictine, ⅓ Cointreau, and ⅓ yellow Chartreuse in that order to create the effect of layers in the finished drink.

ALGONQUIN

2 ounces rye
1 ounce French vermouth
1 ounce pineapple juice

AMARANTH

1 dash bitters
⅔ jigger rye whiskey

Stir, add powdered sugar and fill with carbonated water.

THE BEE-BEE

Dice the skins of citrus fruits, place them in the percolator where the coffee usually goes, pour honey over the diced fruit, and then boil and percolate bourbon over them. This will bring on leprechauns and williwaws after the third cup, we guarantee.

BOURBON LANCER

2 jiggers bourbon
1 lump of sugar
3 dashes of Angostura bitters

Place in large chilled Collins glass with 2 lumps of ice. Fill with chilled champagne. Decorate with lemon peel spiral.

BRAINSTORM

¼ French vermouth
¼ Benedictine
½ best rye whiskey

Stir well with ice and float orange peel on top.

BROWN UNIVERSITY

½ bourbon whiskey
½ French vermouth
2 dashes orange bitters

BURGUNDY CUP

2 jiggers whiskey
1 jigger curaçao
1 jigger Benedictine
1½ bottles Burgundy
1 pint soda water
4 tablespoons sugar

Place in large pitcher with ice cubes and stir. Decorate with slices of orange and pineapple, maraschino cherries, cucumber rind, and fresh mint.

CHAUNCEY

¼ rye whiskey
¼ gin
¼ Italian vermouth
¼ brandy
Dash of orange bitters

CLIQUET

1 jigger bourbon whiskey
Juice of one orange
1 lump of ice
1 dash of rum

Stir instead of shaking.

COLD TODDY

In bottom of an Old-Fashioned glass, crush:

½ teaspoon sugar
1 strip lemon peel, about 1″ long
1 teaspoon water

Add 1 or 2 cubes ice. Pour in 1½-2 ounces your favorite whiskey, give it a quick stir, and there you are. You may add a bit of water or seltzer if you want to last longer.

COLLINS

Sometimes mistakenly labeled John Collins (which is really a gin drink), the whiskey Collins goes like this:

Squeeze the juice of a lemon into a tall glass
Add a heaping teaspoon of sugar
Stir, then add 2 ice cubes or plenty of cracked ice
Pour in a generous jigger of whiskey—bourbon or rye
Fill with cold soda water
Stir with glass swizzle

It is well to stir before each sip, to keep sugar mixed and drink effervescing. Some garnish with cherry, orange slice.

COLUMBIA

1 jigger rye whiskey
1 piece lemon peel
½ lump sugar

Fill with hot water.

COMMODORE

⅓ bourbon whiskey
⅓ crème de cacao
⅓ lemon juice

Dash of grenadine syrup, serve in champagne glass. Tradition can be improved by the use of an electric mixer, with the resultant ice floe similar to that of an Arctic-Tropic Daiquiri.

CONTINENTAL SOUR

(William Penn Hotel, Pittsburgh, Pennsylvania)

1 egg white
1¼ ounces of rye
1¼ ounces fresh lemon juice
1 barspoon sugar

Shake well. Pour into 7-ounce fizz glass, add orange slice, cherry. Then float on top ¼ inch of claret.

COWBOY

⅔ whiskey
⅓ cream

Shake with shaved ice and strain into glass.

CREOLE

½ whiskey
½ sweet vermouth
2 dashes Benedictine
2 Amer Picon

Stir with ice and strain into glass. Serve with twist of lemon peel.

DANNY'S SPECIAL

(Sleepy Hollow Country Club, Tarrytown, N. Y.)

2 ounces bourbon
½ ounce Grand Marnier
1 ounce Cointreau
2 ounces lemon juice

Shake heartily, serve over rocks in a 10-ounce glass.

DOOLITTLE SPECIAL

½ lemon, muddled
3 dashes syrup
1 jigger whiskey

EWING

1 jigger rye whiskey
1 dash of bitters

Stir.

FANCIULLI

½ bourbon whiskey
¼ Italian vermouth
¼ Fernet Branca

Frappé.

FLORIDIAN

⅓ rye whiskey
½ sweet vermouth
1 teaspoonful Amer Picon
½ teaspoonful curaçao
½ teaspoonful sugar
1 dash bitters
Lemon peel
Cracked ice

Shake well and serve.

THE FORESTER

1 maraschino cherry
1 ounce bourbon

⅓ ounce maraschino cherry juice
⅓ ounce lemon juice

Squeeze half a lemon into mixing glass; add five cubes of ice, pour cherry juice, add bourbon; shake well and strain into cocktail glass and decorate with cherry.

FRENCH 95

1 jigger bourbon
⅓ jigger lemon juice
1 teaspoon powdered sugar

Pour into tall glass half full cracked ice, fill with chilled champagne.

FRISCO

2 ounces Benedictine
1 ounce lemon juice
6 ounces rye

Shake with cracked ice.

GLOOM LIFTER

Juice ½ lemon
½ spoon sugar
½ pony raspberry syrup
¼ pony white of egg
1 jigger whiskey
½ teaspoon brandy

GOLDEN GLOW

(New Hotel Jefferson, St. Louis, Missouri)

Mix ½ jigger lemon juice, 1 jigger orange juice, teaspoon sugar, dash of Jamaica rum, 1 jigger bourbon, shaved ice. Strain into glass that has grenadine syrup in its stem.

HARRITY

Dash of bitters
1 dash gin
1 jigger whiskey

HEARNS

⅓ bourbon whiskey
⅓ Italian vermouth
⅓ absinthe (or legal variant)
Dash of bitters (hold your hat)

HIGH HAT

1 ounce Cherry Heering
2 ounces lemon juice
4 ounces rye

Shake with cracked ice.

HONORABLE

⅓ bourbon whiskey
⅓ French vermouth
⅓ Italian vermouth

HORSECAR

1 ounce rye
1 ounce sweet vermouth
1 ounce dry vermouth
2 dashes Angostura

Stir with cracked ice; strain into cocktail glass which may contain maraschino cherry or kumquat.

HORSE'S NECK

Strictly speaking, this is a teetotaler's drink, but add whiskey to the basic and see how it goes:

Peel the whole rind of 1 lemon
Place it in a Collins glass, spiraling up from bottom

and hooking over edge
Add 2 cubes of ice
Fill with cold ginger ale

A dash of bitters is sometimes added to the whiskey.

HOT BRICK

Mix a teaspoon of butter, one teaspoon of sugar and two or three good pinches of cinnamon in the bottom of a glass, adding a jigger of hot water to speed the mixing. Add to this 1 jigger of bourbon. Fill the glass with steaming hot water. Serve and drink while hot.

JAPALAC

1 jigger rye whiskey
1 jigger French vermouth
Juice of ¼ orange
Dash of raspberry syrup

JULEP (1)

(Pendennis Club, Louisville, Kentucky)

Use a 14-ounce or 16-ounce silver julep cup. Dissolve a half of one lump of granulated sugar in clear spring water. Add two or three sprigs of tender mint, place gently (don't bruise the mint). Fill the cup with cracked ice and add 2 full jiggers of bourbon whiskey. Stir gently and refill the julep cup with cracked ice. Take a full bunch of tender mint, cutting the ends to bleed, and place on top. Let it stand for about five minutes before serving. There should be a small linen doily with each julep, as the frost on the cup makes them uncomfortable to hold.

JULEP (2)

(A more minty variety)

Use about 10 sprigs of mint to the glass. Place in a bowl and dust with enough powdered sugar to cover lightly, then add 1 ounce of water for each julep. Macerate thoroughly and let stand for 10 or 15 minutes. Strain through a fine sieve into a glass filled with crushed ice. Fill the glass with fine bourbon, stir thoroughly. Insert a large sprig of mint in each glass and stow in the refrigerator for 30 minutes before serving.

JUNIOR

⅔ rye
Equal parts of lime juice and Benedictine make up balance with dash of bitters

LADDIE'S SUB-BOURBON

2 ounces bourbon
Dash of orange curaçao
Dash of Angostura bitters

Pour over ice in Old-Fashioned glass. Top off with splash of seltzer water.

LAFAYETTE

1 ounce French vermouth
1 ounce Dubonnet

6 ounces rye
1 dash Angostura bitters

Stir and serve over large ice cubes, like an Old-Fashioned in an Old-Fashioned glass.

LIBERAL

½ whiskey
½ Italian vermouth
3 dashes Amer Picon
Dash of orange bitters

Stir.

MANHATTAN (1)

Dash of orange bitters
½ Italian vermouth
½ rye whiskey

Stir. Serve with maraschino cherry.

MANHATTAN (2)

(Town House, Reno, Nevada)

A "special" Manhattan, known in Reno as The Riding Lesson. Stir in iced mixing glass: 3 ounces whiskey, 1 ounce sweet vermouth, 1 drop Angostura bitters, 1 dash Benedictine. Strain into chilled cocktail glass; serve with maraschino cherry.

McCRORY

1 dash bitters
⅔ jigger whiskey
Add powdered sugar

Stir; add charged water.

McKINLEY'S DELIGHT

1 dash absinthe
2 dashes cherry brandy
⅔ whiskey
⅓ Italian vermouth

MILK PUNCH

Into shaker filled with shaved ice put:

1 teaspoon sugar
1 jigger whiskey

Fill glass with milk. Shake. Strain into large goblet or highball glass. Sprinkle with nutmeg.

MILLIONAIRE COCKTAIL

1½ ounces whiskey
½ ounce curaçao
1 dash grenadine
White of 1 egg

Shake with ice as though 7 demons were goading you to it; strain into non-stingy cocktail glass.

MINT JULEP

(In the manner of Irvin S. Cobb)

Take a clean glass and crush a few sprigs of mint with a spoon. Rub the mint all around the inside of the glass, then throw it away. Now fill the glass with finely cracked ice. *Slowly* pour in a measure of bourbon, then add about 2 tablespoons of water in which a lump of sugar has been dissolved. *Do not stir.* Place sprigs of fresh mint in the mouth of the glass.

MONAHAN

Dash of Amer Picon
⅔ whiskey
⅓ Italian vermouth

Stir.

MONTE CARLO

1 jigger rye whiskey
⅓ jigger Benedictine
2 dashes Angostura bitters

Shake well with ice and strain into glass.

MORNING, TEACHER

⅔ jigger whiskey
⅔ jigger brandy
1 dash Pernod
2 dashes bitters
2 dashes curaçao
3 dashes sugar syrup
1 twist lemon peel

Place ingredients in large cocktail glass, with 1-2 pieces of ice. Stir and remove ice. Fill glass with soda water and stir with a teaspoon coated with powdered sugar.

NARRAGANSETT

⅓ Italian vermouth
⅔ whiskey
1 dash anisette

Stir.

NEW ORLEANS

1 jigger bourbon
1 dash orange bitters
2 dashes Angostura bitters
1 dash anisette
2 dashes Pernod
½ lump sugar

Stir well with ice and strain into glass. Serve with twist of lemon peel.

NEW YORK

1½ jiggers rye whiskey
½ teaspoon powdered sugar
1 dash grenadine
Juice of ½ lime
1 twist orange peel

Shake well with ice and strain into glass.

NEW YORKER

1 ounce grenadine
2 ounces lime juice
8 ounces whiskey

Shake with cracked ice. Serve with orange peel.

OLD-FASHIONED (1)

(Sheraton Mount Royal Hotel, Montreal, Canada)

Carefully muddle lump of sugar, dash Angostura bitters, splash of club soda in Old-Fashioned glass. Add 1 ice cube, orange slice, 2 cherries, twist of lemon peel, piece of pineapple, 1½ or 2 ounces of your favorite whiskey. Top with splash of club soda.

OLD-FASHIONED (2)

1 complete lemon peel squeezed into glass
½ teaspoon sugar
½ teaspoon curaçao
2 ounces whiskey

Shake well but do not strain. Serve in glass garnished with slices of pineapple, orange and cherries.

ORDINARY HIGHBALL

1 generous jigger rye whiskey
1 lump of ice

Serve in tall glass with carbonated water.

ORIGINAL OLD-FASHIONED

Muddle ¼ lump of sugar with 2 spoons of water and dash of bitters in bottom of glass. Add 1 lump of ice. Add generous jigger rye whiskey, 1 piece of lemon peel.

PALMER

2 ounces lemon juice
8 ounces bourbon
2 or 3 dashes Angostura bitters

PAN-AMERICAN

1 jigger rye whiskey
½ lemon, muddle
3 dashes syrup

PRINCE

2 dashes orange bitters
1 jigger whiskey
2 dashes crème de menthe on top

Kim Hunter's RAINBOW OLD-FASHIONED

Pour over two ice cubes, 5 teaspoonfuls simple syrup. Add 2 dashes Angostura bitters, 1 teaspoon maraschino cherry juice, 1 maraschino cherry, 2 ounces rye, half a slice of orange, a twist of lemon peel, and half a fresh strawberry. Stir twice gently and serve.

RICKEY

Put several ice cubes in fizz or highball glass.
Squeeze juice of half a lime over ice, then drop lime skin into glass.
Pour in 1 jigger whiskey
Fill with seltzer.

Stir.

ROSEMARY

½ French vermouth
½ whiskey

RYE AND DRY

1 ounce rye
2 or 3 ounces dry vermouth
2 dashes orange bitters

Stir with ice; strain into cocktail glass.

Bob Hope's RYE LEMONADE

1 jigger rye
Mix with fresh lemonade
Add ice

Pour into glass whose rim was rubbed with lemon and sprinkled with sugar and left in refrigerator for at least a half-hour.

RYE FLIP

1 egg
½ spoon sugar
1 jigger rye whiskey

Shake, strain and sprinkle nutmeg on top.

SAZ

For this New Orleans powerhouse, the glass *must* be thoroughly chilled. Put a few drops of Pernod (absinthe without the illegal wormwood) into a large Old-Fashioned glass, then tilt and roll the glass until its inside is thoroughly coated. In a tall mixing glass with several cubes of ice, stir until well chilled:

2 ounces bourbon or rye
3 dashes Peychaud bitters

Then pour, without the ice, into the chilled glass. A lemon peel is sometimes twisted over the top. (Some recipes call for a dash of Italian vermouth, in addition.)

SAZERAC

Crush ½ cube sugar in water. Add 1½ oz. prepared Sazerac, ice cube and after stirring, pour in frappéed cocktail glass.

SEA CAPTAIN'S SPECIAL

In an Old-Fashioned glass place half a lump sugar and douse it with Angostura. Add one and a half jiggers of rye and one lump of ice. Fill the glass with champagne. Top it off with two dashes of true absinthe.

SHERMAN

Dash of bitters
Dash of orange bitters
3 dashes absinthe
⅔ jigger Italian vermouth
⅓ jigger whiskey

SKY CLUB

Juice one orange
1 jigger whiskey; flavored with heavy rum
1 lump ice

Stir.

SOUTHGATE

¼ lump sugar dissolved in one-half pony water
Dash of bitters
1 jigger whiskey
1 piece twisted lemon peel

Carl Carmer's STARS FELL ON ALABAMA COCKTAIL

1 jigger corn whiskey
1 1 dash Peychaud bitters
1 dash Angostura bitters
1 dash Orange Flower Water
1 lump sugar
6 drops absinthe

Ice and stir briskly.

STONE SOUR

½ jigger lemon juice
1 teaspoon crème de menthe
1 jigger bourbon

Into a glass which has been previously filled with chopped

ice and fresh mint sprigs pour the above ingredients. Stir vigorously until glass is frosted. Add 1 maraschino cherry and sparkling water. Sweeten to taste. Insert a small bunch of fresh mint and serve.

SUBURBAN

Dash of orange bitters
Dash of bitters
1/5 port wine
1/5 Jamaica rum
3/5 whiskey

TEMPTATION COCKTAIL

1½ ounces whiskey
½ teaspoon curaçao
½ teaspoon Pernod
½ teaspoon Dubonnet
1 twist orange peel
1 twist lemon peel

Shake well with cracked ice and strain into cocktail glass.

TENNESSEE

2 ounces maraschino
6 ounces rye
1 ounce lemon juice

Shake and serve over cracked ice.

TEN-TON COCKTAIL

2 ounces rye whiskey
1 ounce French vermouth
1 ounce grapefruit juice

Shake well with ice and serve with cherry.

THIS WARD EIGHT

Into a bar glass half filled with broken ice, put

1 teaspoon grenadine
1 ounce rye or bourbon
Juice of ¼ lemon or ½ lime

Shake briskly and strain into cocktail glass. (Some use ½ lemon plus ½ teaspoon sugar. ½ pony of water is sometimes added.)

OR . . . THIS ONE

Juice of 1 lemon
1 barspoon powdered sugar
¾ large whiskey glass bourbon

Dissolve sugar in juice and whiskey. Pour in large glass with a large piece of ice and add:

3 to 4 dashes orange bitters
3 dashes crème de menthe
½ jigger grenadine

Fill glass with seltzer, add

2 slices orange
1 stick pineapple
1 or 2 cherries

THOMPSON

1/3 Italian vermouth
2/3 whiskey
1 piece each of orange peel, pineapple, lemon peel

TORONTO

1 ounce simple syrup
2 ounces Fernet Branca
6 ounces rye whiskey
1 dash Angostura bitters

Stir with large cubes of ice, strain into cocktail glass. Decorate with orange slice.

VIRGINIA JULEP

(A test of patience!)

Pour a measure of bourbon over several sprigs of mint and allow this to stand for half an hour.

Dissolve a teaspoon of sugar in a little water and place in a glass. When half an hour has passed, remove the mint from the whiskey and pour the bourbon into the sugar and water. Pour this mixture back and forth between the two glasses until the liquids are well mixed, then . . . Fill a glass with finely crushed ice and pour the mixture over it. Stir briskly until the frost forms on the glass, then fill the top of the glass with sprigs of fresh mint.

VOLSTEAD

⅓ Swedish Punch
⅓ rye whiskey
⅙ orange juice
⅙ raspberry syrup
1 dash of anisette

WALDORF

Dash of bitters
⅓ whiskey
⅓ absinthe
⅓ Italian vermouth

WHEELER

Juice one-quarter orange
1 jigger French vermouth
1 jigger whiskey
Dash of raspberry syrup

WHISKEY AND MINT

3 sprigs of mint
½ lump sugar; dissolved
Press mint lightly
1 jigger whiskey
Ice

WHISKEY AND TANSY

3 leaves tansy, or
1 pony of tansy mixture
1 jigger whiskey

WHISKEY COOLER

Place in a highball glass 2 jiggers rye or bourbon, the juice of ½ lemon, 1 teaspoon sugar and ice cubes. Fill with chilled ginger ale.

WHISKEY DAISY (I)

1 jigger whiskey
Juice of one-half lemon
3 dashes Cointreau or curaçao
1 teaspoon sugar

Shake with fine ice, strain into 8-ounce highball glass, fizz from siphon. Fruit garnish optional. May be served unstrained, with straws.

WHISKEY DAISY (2)

1 jigger whiskey
Juice of one-half lemon
1 ounce raspberry syrup
½ teaspoon sugar

Shake with fine ice, strain into highball glass, fizz from siphon. Garnish with fruit if you like; fine ice may be kept in instead of strained out.

WHISKEY DAISY (3)

1 jigger whiskey
Juice of one-half lemon

Shake with fine ice, strain into highball glass, fill with sparkling water. Or leave ice in and serve with straw.

WHISKEY SHAKE

Juice of 2 limes
¾ teaspoon sugar
2 ounces whiskey

Shake with great quantities of fine ice; strain into tall flute glass.

WHISKEY SOUR (1)

This is simply a species of fortified lemonade in concentrated form:

1 ounce lemon juice
1 spoonful sugar
3 ounces bourbon or rye

Ice, stir and pour into short glass. Ladies like it decorated with fruit.

WHISKEY SOUR (2)

1 jigger rye whiskey
½ juice of lemon
½ spoon sugar
1 lump of ice

WHISKEY SOUR IN THE ROUGH

(*Hotel Flamingo, Las Vegas, Nevada*)

In large mixing glass, muddle 1 spoon sugar with 2 quarters each of fresh orange and lemon. Fill glass with cracked ice, add 2 ounces bourbon. Shake and pour into mixing glass.

WHITE SHADOW

⅓ rye whiskey
⅓ Pernod
⅓ cream
1 pinch nutmeg

Shake well with shaved ice and strain into glass.

WRIGHT BROTHERS

6 jiggers rye
6 jiggers port
Juice of 3 lemons
4 teaspoons sugar

Shake in a shaker with cracked ice, then add the beaten whites of 3 eggs. Shake for another few moments, then pour into cocktail glass in which a cube of pineapple has been placed.

YASHMAK

⅓ rye whiskey
⅓ Pernod
⅓ dry vermouth
1 dash Angostura bitters
1 or 2 pinches sugar

Stir well with ice and strain into glass.

SCOTCH

ARTIST'S SPECIAL
(Artist Bar, Rue Pigalle, Paris)

⅓ Scotch whisky
⅓ sherry
⅙ lemon juice
⅙ Groseille syrup

THE BAIRN

⅔ Scotch whisky
⅓ Cointreau
1 dash orange bitters

BARBARY COAST

1 ounce each of:

Scotch
Gin
Rum
Crème de cacao
Cream

Briskly shaken and strained.

BENEDICT

⅓ Scotch whisky
⅓ Benedictine
⅓ ginger ale

BILL ORR

2 jiggers Scotch whisky
Juice of small orange
1 dash of orange bitters

BLOOD & SAND

Equal parts of:

Scotch
Cherry brandy
Orange juice
Sweet vermouth

BLUE BLAZER

1 jigger Scotch or rye
1 lump sugar
Very hot water

Set liquid on fire and pour from one glass to another. Twist of lemon peel on top.

BORDEN CHASE

¾ Scotch whisky
¼ Italian vermouth
1 dash of orange bitters
1 dash of Pernod or Oxygene

BUNNY HUG

1/3 gin
1/3 Scotch whisky
1/3 absinthe

BYRRH COCKTAIL

1/3 French vermouth
1/3 Scotch whisky
1/3 Byrrh

CAMERON'S KICK

1/3 Scotch whisky
1/3 Irish whiskey
1/6 lemon juice
1/6 Orgeat (almond) syrup

CARIBBEAN JOY

(Caribbean Club, Key Largo, Florida)

Shake, with ice, 1 1/2 ounces Scotch, juice of 1 lime, 1 barspoon powdered sugar, and 2 dashes of Cointreau. Serve in 4- or 5-ounce cocktail glass.

CHANCELLOR COCKTAIL

2/3 Scotch whisky
1/6 French vermouth
1/6 port wine
1 dash of bitters

CHURCHILL

1/2 Scotch

Cointreau, Italian vermouth and lime juice equally represented in other half.

THE COMFORTER

(Chambord, New York, N. Y.)

2/3 Scotch
1/3 lemon juice
1/2 teaspoon sugar
Dash of Cointreau

FRANCES ANN

(Beverly Hills Hotel, Beverly Hills, California)

Combine in mixing glass, 1 ounce Scotch, 1/2 ounce Cherry Heering, 1/2 ounce dry vermouth. Stir well until chilled. Serve in king-size cocktail glass.

THE GASLIGHT

(Billy's, New York City)

1 1/2 ounces of Scotch
1/2 ounce Italian vermouth
Dash of orange curaçao

Shake well and pour over the rocks in a goblet. Garnish with a twist of orange skin, a thimbleful of Drambuie. Pour Drambuie carefully over chilled surface of drink.

GENTLE JOHN

1 jigger Scotch whisky
1 dash of orange bitters, French vermouth and Cointreau

GLAMIS
(pronounced Glarms)

1/2 Scotch whisky
1/2 Calisaya bitters

GLASGOW

½ Scotch whisky
½ French vermouth
3 dashes absinthe
3 dashes bitters

Ice and shake well.

THE HEATHER

⅔ Scotch whisky
2 dashes of French vermouth
1 dash of Angostura bitters

HIGHLAND BITTERS

Grind in a mortar the following:

1¾ ounces gentian root
½ ounce orange peel
1 ounce coriander seed
¼ ounce camomile flowers
½ ounce cloves
¼ ounce cinnamon

Add this to two bottles of Scotch. Let it stand two weeks, sealed, in a crockery jar. Then drink.

HIGHLAND COCKTAIL

½ Italian vermouth
½ Scotch whisky
1 dash of bitters

HOLE-IN-ONE

2 ounces Scotch
1 ounce French vermouth
Dash of lemon juice
Dash of orange bitters

JOHN McCLAIN

1 jigger Scotch
1 teaspoon syrup
2 dashes of bitters

L. G. COCKTAIL

1 glass Scotch whisky
Followed by one glass beer

MAMIE TAYLOR

Squeeze ½ lime into Collins glass
Add 2 cubes of ice
Pour in 1 jigger Scotch
Fill with cold ginger ale

MODERN COCKTAIL

⅓ Scotch whisky
½ sloe gin
1 dash orange bitters
1 dash absinthe
4 dashes gum syrup

MORNING GLORY FIZZ

1 white of egg
1 teaspoon of sugar
1 juice of lemon
1 glass of Scotch whisky
1 teaspoon of Oxygene

Shake well and pour into large glass, fill to top with soda.

POLLY'S SPECIAL COCKTAIL

1 ounce Scotch
½ ounce Cointreau
½ ounce grapefruit juice

Shake with cracked ice; strain into chilled cocktail glass.

REMSEN COOLER

Put peel of whole lemon in large glass with two lumps of ice. Add glass of Scotch whisky and fill with soda.

ROBBER COCKTAIL

⅔ Scotch whisky
⅓ Italian vermouth
Dash of bitters

Serve in cocktail glass with cherry.

ROB ROY (1)

2 parts Scotch whisky
1 part Italian vermouth
1 dash of bitters

ROB ROY (2)

(Waldorf-Astoria Hotel, New York City)

To 2 ounces of Scotch add ½ ounce of dry vermouth. (For more than one drink, maintain 4-1 ratio.) Stir with cracked ice and add twist of lemon peel. Serve in chilled cocktail glass.

SCOTCH COOLER

Place in a highball glass 1 or 2 jiggers Scotch whisky, 3 dashes crème de menthe and ice cubes. Fill with chilled soda water.

SCOTCH MIST

1 jigger Scotch

Shake with finely shaved ice. Serve unstrained in Old-Fashioned glass. Add twist of lemon peel. Can be served with short straws.

STONE FENCE (1)

Place 2 jiggers Scotch whisky and 2 dashes Peychaud's bitters in a highball glass with 1 small twist of lemon peel and ice cubes. Fill with soda water.

STONE FENCE (2)

1 jigger of Scotch whisky in large glass
1 lump of ice

Fill with cider.

Garry Moore's SCOTCH MILK PUNCH

Shake thoroughly 2 ounces Scotch and 6 ounces milk with sugar and ice. Pour into highball glass, and sprinkle drink with nutmeg.

SCOTCH OLD-FASHIONED

Substitute Scotch whisky for bourbon or rye in the Old-Fashioned recipe, page 138. Occasional Scotch drinkers like it, but an earnest Scotch-lover's reaction will be, "You've ruined some mighty fine Scotch."

SCOTCH SAZ

1 jigger Scotch whisky
1 teaspoon Italian vermouth
1 dash of absinthe or Oxygene

SCOTCH SMASH

(Occidental Restaurant, Washington, D. C.)

Muddle ½ lump sugar with 3 sprigs mint in Old-Fashioned glass. Put in 1 ice cube, 1½ ounces Scotch, add soda. Stir and trim with fruit.

SCOTCH SOUR

(The Recess Club, Detroit, Michigan)

Combine in shaker 2 ounces Scotch, juice of ½ lime, teaspoon powdered sugar. Strain into 8-ounce glass, add a little club soda, decorate with orange slices and cherry.

TOM JOHNSTONE

½ Scotch whisky
⅙ lime juice
⅙ Italian vermouth
⅙ Cointreau

TRINITY

½ Scotch whisky
⅓ French vermouth
1 dash of crème de menthe
1 dash of orange bitters
1 dash of apricot brandy

TRYST COCKTAIL

⅓ Scotch whisky
⅓ Parfait d'Amour
⅓ Italian vermouth
2 dashes absinthe
2 dashes of orange bitters

WALTERS

½ Scotch whisky
¼ orange juice
¼ lemon juice

WOODWARD

⅓ Scotch whisky
⅓ grapefruit juice
⅓ French vermouth

TEQUILA

MARGARITA COCKTAIL

1 ounce tequila
Dash of Triple Sec
Juice of ½ lime or lemon

Pour over crushed ice, stir. Rub the rim of a stem glass with rind of lemon or lime, spin in salt—pour and sip.

PRADO COCKTAIL

(Hotel Del Prado, Mexico City)

Shake well, with cracked ice, 1½ ounces white tequila, juice of ½ lemon, ⅓ white of egg, ⅓ ounce maraschino, dash of grenadine. Strain into sour glass. Garnish with lemon slice, cherry.

TEQUILA SOUR

1 ounce sugar syrup
2 ounces lemon juice
8 ounces tequila

Decorate with cherry.

VODKA

BANANA PUNCH

(Chasen's, Beverly Hills, California)

Into a Collins glass filled with crushed ice, pour a mixture of 1 jigger vodka, 1 dash Abricotine, juice of ½ lime. Top with splash of club soda and sprigs of mint.

BLOODY MARY

1 jigger vodka
2 jiggers tomato juice
⅓ jigger lemon juice
1 dash Worcestershire sauce
Salt and pepper to taste

Shake well with ice and strain into glass.

BLUE MONDAY

¾ vodka
¼ Cointreau
1 dash blue vegetable extract (coloring)

Stir well with ice and strain into glass. Coloring may be omitted.

GYPSY

⅔ vodka
⅓ Benedictine
1 dash of bitters

THE HUNTSMAN

(Café Nino, New York City)

1 jigger vodka
4 dashes of Jamaica rum
Juice of ½ lime
Sugar to taste

Shake well and strain. Pour into cocktail glass.

KANGAROO

1 jigger vodka
½ jigger dry vermouth

Stir with cracked ice and strain into glass. Serve with twist of lemon peel.

KRETCHMA COCKTAIL

⅖ vodka
⅖ cremè de cacao
⅕ lemon juice
1 dash grenadine

MOSCOW MULE (1)

Put the juice of ½ lime and the rind into a 10-ounce glass or mug. Add 2 ounces vodka, 2 cubes of ice and fill with ginger ale. Stir and serve.

MOSCOW MULE (2)

(Wonder Palms Hotel, Palm Springs, California)

Put 1 jigger vodka, juice of ½ lime and 2 ice cubes into copper mug. Fill mug with ginger beer. Garnish with remainder of the lime. Add a thin strip of cucumber and serve.

NINOTCHKA

(Two Guitars, New York City)

⅓ crème de cacao
Jigger of vodka
⅓ lemon juice

RUSSIAN

1 jigger vodka
1 jigger dry gin
1 jigger crème de cacao

Stir well with ice and strain into glass.

RUSSIAN BEAR

½ vodka
¼ crème de cacao
¼ cream

Stir well with ice and strain into glass.

SCREWDRIVER

In 6-ounce glass, place 2 cubes of ice. Add 2 ounces vodka. Fill balance of glass with orange juice and stir.

TOVARICH

1 jigger vodka
⅔ jigger Kümmel
Juice of ½ lime

Shake with cracked ice and strain into glass.

THE TWISTER

1½ ounces vodka over 3 cubes of ice. Juice of ⅓ lime, drop in rind. Fill glass with Seven-Up and serve in tall glass.

VODKA

1 jigger vodka
½ jigger cherry brandy
Juice of ½ lemon or lime

Shake with ice and strain into glass.

VODKA GIBSON

2 jiggers vodka
½ jigger dry vermouth

Stir well with ice and strain into glass. Serve with pickled pearl onion.

Nancy Berg's VODKA ICEBERG

1 jigger vodka on rocks
Dash of Pernod

VODKA MARTINI

4 or 5 ounces vodka
1 ounce dry vermouth

Stir well with ice and strain into glass. Serve with a twist of lemon peel.

VODKA SLING

(Serves 6)

8 jiggers vodka
2 jiggers Benedictine
2 jiggers cherry brandy
Juice of 2 lemons
1 teaspoon Angostura bitters
1 teaspoon orange bitters

Shake well with ice and strain into glass. Fill with chilled soda water and garnish with fruit, if desired.

VODKA-ON-THE-ROCKS

Fill Old-Fashioned glass with ice cubes. Fill with vodka as desired, and serve with a twist of lemon peel.

VOLGA BOATMAN

1 jigger vodka
1 jigger cherry brandy
1 jigger orange juice

Stir well with ice and strain into glass.

WINES

ADDINGTON

½ sweet vermouth
½ dry vermouth

Stir well with ice and strain into large cocktail glass. Fill with soda water and serve with twist of lemon peel.

ADONIS (1)

1 ounce Italian vermouth
2 ounces dry sherry
2 dashes Angostura bitters

Stir briefly over ice cubes.

ADONIS (2)

⅔ dry sherry
⅓ sweet vermouth
1 dash orange bitters

Stir well with ice and strain into glass.

ALFONSO COCKTAIL

½ jigger Dubonnet
1 cube ice
1 dash bitters
1 lump sugar

Place the sugar in a large saucer champagne glass and sprinkle with bitters. Add ice and Dubonnet and fill with iced champagne. Serve with twist of lemon peel.

AMERICAN BEAUTY COCKTAIL

1 ounce muscatel, 4 ounces champagne, thoroughly chilled and garnished with a large grape.

THE AMERICANO

3 ounces Italian vermouth
Dash of bitters
Slice of lemon peel
Seltzer as desired

Serve in a small highball glass or goblet.

ARISE MY LOVE

Put 1 teaspoon crème de menthe in a champagne glass, then fill with champagne.

BAHIA COCKTAIL

1 dash Angostura bitters
1 ounce dry vermouth
1 ounce sherry
¼ ounce Pernod

Stir well in cracked ice and strain into cocktail glass. Twist lemon peel over drink.

BAMBOO COCKTAIL

1 jigger sherry
1 jigger dry vermouth
2 dashes Angostura

Stir with ice, strain into stem glass, add green olive or pearl onion.

BISHOP

In a large bar glass place 2 dashes of lime juice, 1 tablespoon of sugar, ½ orange squeezed, and ½ of water. Fill glass ¾ full with shaved ice, then fill to the top with Burgundy. Add a few drops of Jamaica rum and stir with a spoon. Serve with a straw.

BISHOP'S COOLER

2 dashes Angostura bitters
½ ounce lemon juice
1 ounce orange juice
1 teaspoonful fine granulated sugar
3 ounces Burgundy
½ ounce Jamaica rum

Make this drink in a 10-ounce Collins glass. Add sufficient fine ice to fill glass and stir.

BRAZIL

½ sherry
½ dry vermouth
1 dash Pernod
1 dash Angostura bitters

Stir well with ice and strain into glass. Squeeze lemon peel over top.

BROOKLYN

1 ounce French vermouth
3 ounces rye
1 dash maraschino
1 dash Amer Picon

Stir and serve over large ice cubes.

BUGHOUSE

1 ounce Italian vermouth
3 ounces cognac
1 teaspoonful absinthe

Stir.

BURGUNDY OR CLARET CUP

To each bottle of claret or Burgundy add one bottle of club soda, one glass of sherry, one pony Triple Sec, and one pony of brandy; also the rind of one lemon cut very thin; powdered sugar to taste. Decorate with fresh pineapple, orange, and one slice of fresh cucumber rind. Let brew a short time before serving, then add a boulder of ice and, if available, a flock of fresh mint. Fresh raspberries or peaches optional in season.

BYRRH—CASSIS

1 glass Byrrh
½ glass Cassis
Balance soda water

CECIL PICK-ME-UP

Shake well one yolk of egg, one glass of brandy, and one teaspoon of castor sugar. Strain into medium sized wineglass and fill balance with champagne.

CHAMPAGNE CUP

To one bottle of champagne and two bottles of charged water, add one wine glass of brandy and one of curaçao, one large spoonful of sugar. Chill thoroughly and serve.

CHAMPAGNE COCKTAIL (1)

(Chambord, New York City)

Serve in Burgundy glass: start with prechilled glass, ½ lump sugar, dash of Angostura bitters. Add ½ teaspoon cognac, twist of lemon peel. Fill with iced champagne.

CHAMPAGNE COCKTAIL (2)

Take a nice full-blown lemon and from it scrape off as much of the yellow as you can with a cube of sugar. Place the sweet in a champagne glass with a small lump of ice, add a dash of Angostura bitters and slowly fill the glass with champagne, stirring it only enough to dissolve the sugar. Serve with a twist of lemon peel.

CHAMPAGNE FIZZ

Place the juice of 1 orange in a highball glass with several ice cubes. Fill with iced champagne.

CHAMPAGNE JULEP

Put one lump of sugar, one sprig of fresh mint, and one lump of ice in a large, fancy wineglass. Then pour champagne very slowly, stirring gently all the time, and ornament the top with fruit in season.

CHAMPAGNE PICK-ME-UP

Shake well one liqueur of brandy, one liqueur of French vermouth, and one teaspoonful of gum syrup. Strain into wineglass, and add champagne.

CHAMPAGNE VELVET

Half fill a tall glass with iced stout. Fill with iced champagne as desired. Pour very slowly or glass will overflow.

CLARET, SHERRY, OR PORT LEMONADE

In a large bar glass put ½ tablespoon sugar and 5 or 6 dashes of lemon juice. Fill glass ¾ way with shaved ice. Pour on one wineglass of desired wine. Fill to top with water. Dress with fresh fruit.

CLARET WINE COBBLER

¾ tablespoon sugar
Juice of 1 orange

1½ wineglasses claret

Mix and top with a little port.

COUNTRY CLUB COOLER

2 jiggers dry vermouth
1 teaspoon grenadine

Place in tall glass with ice and fill with chilled soda water.

CUPID

2 jiggers sherry
1 egg
1 teaspoon powdered sugar
1 pinch cayenne pepper

Shake well with ice and strain into glass.

Ernest Hemingway's DEATH IN THE AFTERNOON COCKTAIL

Pour 1 jigger of absinthe into a champagne glass. Add iced champagne until it attains the proper opalescent milkiness. Drink 3 to 5 of these slowly.

DIAMOND COCKTAILS

(Serves 4)

Juice of one lime, one lemon, one orange, four tablespoons of raspberry syrup, one wineglass of gin. Mix and divide into four tall glasses filled with cracked ice. Then fill to the top with champagne.

DR. PITCHER'S PARCH REMEDY

8 slices of orange, cut into halves
4 slices of lemon similarly bisected
2 bottles sauterne

Stir together in glass pitcher, adding sugar if desired, and let stand in refrigerator about an hour to allow flavors to fraternize. Serve iced, with sprigs of mint nosegaying top of pitcher.

DUBONNET

1 glass Dubonnet
½ glass lemon syrup
Balance soda water

DUKE OF MARLBOROUGH

½ sherry
½ sweet vermouth
3 dashes raspberry syrup
Juice of 1 lime

Shake well with ice and strain into glass.

FIG LEAF

1 jigger sweet vermouth
⅔ jigger light rum
Juice of ½ lime
1 dash Angostura bitters

Shake well with ice and strain into glass.

FIVE O'CLOCK IN SANDUSKY

1 cup strong tea, cold
2 bottles Catawba wine
2 ounces brandy
1 ounce maraschino liqueur
1 bottle sparkling water

Sweeten to taste. Decorate with sliced fruit and berries in season. Serve in punch bowl containing large lump of ice.

FRENCH VERMOUTH AND CURACAO

1 glass French vermouth
½ glass curaçao
Balance soda water

GOLDEN FRAPPE

1 cup orange juice
2 tablespoons lemon juice
2 tablespoons sugar
1 cup white port

Stir until sugar is dissolved, then pour over finely crushed ice into tall tumbler.

GRAND SLAM

½ Swedish Punch
¼ sweet vermouth
¼ dry vermouth

Stir well with ice and strain into glass.

HOT MINT BURGUNDY DELIGHT

6 fresh crisp mint leaves
1 piece lemon peel
1 tablespoon sugar
3 ounces Burgundy

Muddle well together and add a few drops of maraschino cherry juice syrup, one small stick of cinnamon and two whole cloves. Then add 3 ounces of Burgundy and an equal amount of hot water. Stir and serve.

ITALIAN WINE LEMONADE

Pour in a large bar glass ½ wineglass raspberry syrup, ¼ wineglass of Orgeat syrup, 3 or 4 dashes of lemon juice. Fill glass ¾ way with shaved ice. Add 1 wineglass of claret or port and fill balance with water. Mix well and garnish with fresh fruit.

KISS LIKE WINE

½ French vermouth
½ Dubonnet

MIMOSA

Use large champagne glass; fill it with equal parts of chilled champagne and freshly squeezed orange juice.

THE ORLENA

Put one lump of sugar in a wineglass. Soak it with absinthe and add one lump of ice. Fill the glass with champagne, and add a dash of brandy on top with a piece of lemon peel.

Art Linkletter's PAPAYA COCKTAIL

2 ounces Papaya juice
1 ounce sherry

Serve in cocktail glass.

PEACH BOWL

Pour one teaspoon of peach brandy into a chilled goblet. Peel a fresh, firm, ripe peach, pierce with silver fork on entire surface, using care not to bruise. Place the peach in the glass and fill with chilled champagne.

PEACH VELVET

(Savoy-Plaza, New York City)

Four ounces champagne
Dash peach brandy
Peeled sliced peach
Four pieces cracked ice.

PHILADELPHIA COOLER

Fill two large glasses with cracked ice, add mint (small amount) and two lumps of sugar to each. Divide one pint of champagne between the two, pouring the wine on top of the crushed ice.

PORT FLIP

Two eggs, cracked on the rim of a shaker, two teaspoons sugar, one cup of port, much, much cracked ice; shaken dementedly. Pour into two Delmonico glasses or fair-sized goblets. Freckle with nutmeg.

PORT WINE PUNCH (1)

Dissolve in a little water ½ tablespoon of sugar, 1 or 2 dashes of lemon juice and the juice of ½ orange. Fill glass with shaved ice and mix in well with spoon 1½ wineglasses of port wine. Ornament with fruit. A large bar glass is used.

PORT WINE PUNCH (2)

Mix well in a large bar glass ½ tablespoon of sugar, ½ tablespoon of Orgeat syrup, 1 or 2 dashes of lemon juice and ½ wineglass of water. Fill glass with shaved ice and 1½ wineglasses of port. Stir and dress with fresh fruit.

RHINE WINE COBBLER

1½ tablespoon sugar, ½ wineglass of water, and 1½ wineglasses of Rhine wine. Mix and serve.

SAUTERNE CUP

Put big lumps of ice in a glass pitcher, pour in:

1 quart sauterne
1 pint soda
1 wineglass sherry
1 pony brandy

Add:

Rind of one lemon
3 slices orange
3 slices lemon
1 slice cucumber peel
Any fresh berries available

Stir and serve in tall glasses ornamented with fruit. Or substitute champagne for sauterne, add 1 pony white curaçao and use fresh mint instead of fruit.

SENSATION

2 ounces port wine
1 ounce brandy
Twist of lemon peel

Stir well and serve.

SHERRY AND BITTERS

Roll a dash of bitters to cover inside of wineglass. Fill glass with sherry.

SHERRY COBBLER

Dissolve in a large bar glass ½ tablespoon sugar in a little water and a pony of pineapple syrup. Fill glass with shaved ice and pour on 1½ wineglasses of sherry, stir well and add a little port. Garnish with fresh fruit.

SHERRY COCKTAIL

2 ounces dry sherry, prechilled
2 ounces French vermouth, prechilled

SHERRY AND EGG

Pour in a whiskey glass enough sherry to cover the bottom to prevent the egg from sticking to the glass. Break into this an ice-cold egg. Add the amount of sherry desired.

SHERRY FLIP (1)

Shake with ice 1 egg, 1 teaspoon granulated sugar and 2 ounces sherry. Strain into Delmonico glass and dust with grated nutmeg.

SHERRY FLIP (2)

(Pump Room, Ambassador East, Chicago, Illinois)

In your electric mixer: 1½ ounces sherry, ½ cup shaved ice, heaping teaspoon granulated sugar, white and yolk of an egg, 3 dashes crème de cacao. Mix well. Pour into well-chilled 5½ ounce champagne cocktail glass. Top with two or three pinches of nutmeg.

SHERRY OLD-FASHIONED

With the full trappings of an Old-Fashioned—the lump of sugar, thrice shot with Angostura and muddled till dissolved; twist of lemon epidermis, double jigger sherry, ice cube or two; maraschino cherry, orange slice, glass baton; and serve pronto before the melting of the ice undermines authority.

SHERRY WINE PUNCH

Pour into large bar glass ½ wineglass of Orgeat syrup, and 1 or 2 dashes of lemon juice. Fill glass with shaved ice. Then pour in 1½ wineglasses of sherry while stirring. Dress with fresh fruit and float on a little claret.

SIR CHARLES PUNCH

(Christmas)

Fill a large tumbler half full with shaved ice. Add to this one teaspoon of granulated sugar, one wineglass of port, ½ glass of brandy, ½ glass of curaçao. Stir well with a spoon. Ornament the top with slices of orange, pineapple, and split grapes.

SOUL KISS

1/3 dry vermouth
1/3 sweet vermouth
1/6 Dubonnet
1/6 orange juice

Stir well with ice and strain into glass.

SOYER AU CHAMPAGNE

(One of the most popular drinks at Christmas in the continental cafés)

Take a large tumbler and in the bottom put two large tablespoons of vanilla ice cream. Add 2 dashes of Maraschino, 2 dashes of curaçao, 2 dashes of brandy, then fill to the top with champagne. Stir and add a slice of pineapple, a slice of orange, a slice of lemon, 2 cherries and 2 strawberries.

SPRITZER

1/3 Rhine wine
2/3 seltzer

Pour chilled wine into highball glass, add well chilled seltzer and stir lightly.

THE SUNSET LIMITED

2 jiggers muscatel
Juice of half a lemon
Ice cubes
2 dashes Angostura
Couple of squirts of seltzer
Fill glass with chablis

Stir lightly—mint sprig trimming, if available

SUN VALLEY SPECIAL

This drink is none other than the old continental standby, vermouth straight, served in a new manner in the distinctive new Italian vermouth glass—a 4½-inch stemless goblet which rises, four-sided and four-cornered, in a shapely crescendo from a square base. The inventory discloses 3 ounces of Italian vermouth, 2 cubes of ice, twist of lemon peel, a straddled slice of orange, and a cherry pierced with a paper-featherered arrow, demonstrating that the William Tell school of fruit shooting has made progress.

SWISS

1 ounce Dubonnet
1 ounce Kirsch

Stir with cubes. Serve with lemon twist.

TROCADERO

½ dry vermouth
½ sweet vermouth
1 dash grenadine
1 dash orange bitters

Stir well with ice and strain into glass. Add cherry and squeeze lemon peel over top.

UPSTAIRS

2 jiggers Dubonnet
Juice of ¼ lemon

Pour into large cocktail glass with ice cubes and fill with soda water.

VERMOUTH

2 ounces Italian vermouth
1 teaspoon Amer Picon
½ teaspoon curaçao
1 dash bitters
1 lemon peel
1 small sprig mint
½ teaspoon sugar

Shake well with cracked ice, and serve with cherry.

VERMOUTH CASSIS
(Fairmont Hotel, San Francisco, California)

In 8-ounce Collins glass, drop three cubes of ice, pour in 1½ ounces dry vermouth, 1 ounce Crème de Cassis, fill glass with club soda. Note: do *not* use crushed ice, stir lightly. Drink is at its best when highly carbonated.

VERMOUTH CASSIS
(The English Way)

½ Italian vermouth
½ French vermouth

Serve cold with a twist of lemon peel.

VERMOUTH SPECIAL

½ teaspoon sugar
1 lemon peel squeezed into glass
1 dash bitters
1 sprig mint
½ teaspoon curaçao
1 teaspoon Amer Picon
2 ounces Italian vermouth
1 ounce whiskey

Shake well with ice, strain, serve.

WALSH'S CHAMPAGNE COCKTAIL

Use 10-ounce glass. Fill with cracked ice.

1 lump sugar
1 sprig mint
Lemon peel
Fill glass to brim with champagne
Serve with cherry

WINE COLLINS

Squeeze juice of ½ lemon into Collins glass, fill to halfway mark with any table wine. Add ice cubes, fill with sparkling water and stir. Sugar may be added to lemon juice if desired.

LEARN YOUR AFTER-MATH

This chapter calls for what is a Bold Stand.

We do not propose—as some of our estimable friends in business might wish us to—to ignore the fact that if you drink too much, you get drunk. And if you get awfully drunk, you get desperately sick. And this sickness brings you apparently so close to Death that you may even hope for a visit from the Dark Destroyer himself.

Nor do we propose—as some of our other estimable friends in good faith might wish us to—to deride the drinking of all liquor, to say that the morning after will teach you, and even that temperance in everything is great. Temperance? Temperance in love? Temperance in music—no high C, no low B-flat? Temperance in speed—never over 50? Temperance—for what? No. Rather would we say that you must live within your excesses and pay for them, if you can, since you *must.*

"Oh, that second bottle," the Earl of Rochester wrote to Henry Savile two centuries ago, "it is the sincerest, wisest, and most impartial downright friend we have, tell the truth, of ourselves, and forces us to speak truth of others; banishes flattery from our tongues and distrust from our hearts; sets us above the mean policy of Court-Prudence, which makes us lie to each other all day, for fear of being betrayed by each other all night."

So you would want moderation in everything? Be moderate then, and die moderately early. But remember well that the oldsters who live to more than a hundred look out of their wise merry eyes at the reporters and always say: "It's because

I didn't marry, or because I smoked ten cigars a day, or because I drink a bottle a day." They don't really mean that they did just this: but what they mean is, that they stayed alive because they found something worth doing more than just a little. There's your therapy for you.

Alcohol, to put it so bluntly that we are sure to collect a passel of critics, is no enemy of man. It is, in fact, a necessary part of his blood stream. A man normally has .003 per cent alcohol in his blood stream, and he gets this by the action of his gastric juices on the sugars and starches he consumes. We hate to say this to certain blue-nosed people, but even they have a little still in them—making alcohol every minute—and no law can legislate it out of existence. Thus, it will not physically damage any of the organs in the body: heart, liver, kidneys, brain, stomach, or nervous system. But—if you insist—if you hoist that .003 to .7 per cent you're dead.

But there's truth in everything, and more untruth about hangovers than ever you can shake a swizzle stick at. We have studied this thing, believe us. And we'll bet that some of the things you're about to hear as untrue are your very own favorite sayings. But stand by: you're wrong. Listen.

1. Alcohol does not bring on cirrhosis of the liver. It is true that more sufferers are also drinkers: that is simply because there are more drinkers than non-drinkers.

2. Alcohol is not good for snake bite or heat prostration. In fact, it is very bad.

3. Alcohol does not warm the body. Its actual effect is the exact opposite.

4. Alcohol is not a stimulant: it is a sedative.

5. Alcohol, in itself, does not produce fat.

6. Mixing drinks will not get you drunker than if you stick to one kind.

With this philosophical, theosophical, and argumentative start, let us launch you into an essay by Don Williams, entitled "Hamstringing the Hangover," which our researches compel us to declare is quite authoritative.

"Few afflictions are more horrible than a really first-rate hangover—one with long matted hair and a guttural voice. One of the few things more horrible is the hangover remedy which each well-intentioned friend forces down your gullet the morning after.

"The hangover is a malady without a country. Scientists have never accorded it a professional standing. The attitude of the medical profession, apparently, is that you have made your own hangover so you can groan in it.

"The truth of the matter is that no one has ever gone to the trouble of finding out exactly what a hangover is.

"This much has been learned: All the commonly known treatments (with one or two exceptions) only make the hangover worse.

"The Hair of the Dog, as we shall see, is a downright assassin; most of the rest have just enough truth in them to be plausible —and enough untruth to make them poisonous.

"To prevent mass suicide by readers at this point, let it be stated here there is one way to beat a hangover. It is the result of research on the part of an anonymous group of physicians—perhaps the first serious study ever made on the subject. The method requires fortitude, however, and to explain its logic we must first examine into the matter of what happens when, driven by despair, joy, or just plain boredom, a fairly human being steps up to the bar and says, 'A quick one, Joe.'

"Alcohol, when tossed into an unsuspecting stomach, behaves as no other poison does. It goes directly into the blood stream, without being affected chemically by any of the digestive juices. The walls of the stomach suck up about one-third of the pure alcohol in your rye highball almost before the bartender has time to ring up the sale. The remaining two-thirds is absorbed by the intestinal walls, generally within an hour of the time you first bend your elbow.

"Once in the blood stream, alcohol acts both as a narcotic and an anesthetic. First of all, it has the narcotic effect of relaxing the walls of the blood vessels. This causes increased heart action and a rise of skin temperature. Hence the warm glow of the first or second drink.

"Next alcohol has an anesthetic quality which is entirely unique. Carried in the blood stream to the capillaries of the brain, its first act is to put to sleep the so-called inhibitory centers. It gives them a shot of ether (for, as a matter of fact, alcohol and ether are closely allied chemically). The inhibitory centers of the brain are the watchdogs of our conduct—something akin to the 'conscience' of which moralists speak. With them safely asleep, our worries disappear, our sense of responsibility vanishes, and our shortcomings are forgotten. Hence the 'lift.'

"But alcohol does not stop its anesthetizing at the brain. It continues to creep about the body with its little can of ether putting the various motor centers to sleep. The knees become wobbly. Speech becomes thick.

"Here is the important fact: A concentration of 0.25 per cent or more of alcohol in the blood brings about a pretty general sleepiness of all the organs.

"We have arrived, then, at an understanding of an old saw: When you become 'paralyzed drunk,' all of your organs, actually and technically are paralyzed.

"We will attempt no detailed explanation of the whys of a hangover beyond this fact. The parched tongue and the dry gullet which scream for a flood of ice water; the head which feels like one of Dr. Picard's ill-fated balloons; the sickening conviction that one's stomach has turned into a lump of cold whale fat; the sensation so aptly described by a fiction writer of 'being actually about one step to the left and five feet above one's own physical body,' and the frightening taste which makes one suspect he has been sitting up the entire night licking Lithuanian postage stamps—none of these symptoms has ever been thoroughly diagnosed in the laboratory.

"One fact, only, is known with certainty: Much of your morning-after misery is due to the anesthetizing after effects of ethyl alcohol. Or, to put it more simply, to the fact that you and all your organs are still partially paralyzed.

"What happens, then, when our unhappy victim, awakening with all these dread symptoms, rushes to the kitchen, gulps two glasses of ice water, downs a Prairie Oyster, quaffs a tomato juice cocktail and then completes this fearful ritual by swilling four cups of black coffee? What happens? Are you asking me? At the very best, he departs for the office with the vague hope that he will be run down by a truck, struck by lightning, or become accidentally involved in a Chinese tong war.

"He is in such a state that he believes nothing could possibly make his condition worse. Consequently, he is fresh meat for all the hangover specialists in town. And he is not long in falling into their hands.

"The elevator boy says, with a smirk, 'So you flung one last night, did you, Mr. Blop?'

" 'Uh,' our Mr. Blop confesses.

" 'Try a Flippant Hen,' the boy suggests. Mr. Blop looks at him blankly.

" 'You know,' the boy confides. 'An egg in a short glass of beer. It's the McCoy for a hangover. Shall I take you back down to get one?'

"Poor Mr. Blop hasn't the strength to argue. He surrenders.

"The Flippant Hen clucks and cackles in his paralyzed stomach. For a few tense moments Mr. Blop has hopes. Then the Hen suddenly rolls over and gurgles to her death in the pool of tomato juice, tobasco, ice water and black coffee. Mr. Blop is forced to swallow rapidly to keep alive.

"In rapid succession, determined friends dose him with aspirin, which only makes him more sleepy; with a 'Spirit of '76' (teaspoon of spirits of ammonia in a bromo), which makes his ears ring for a few minutes and then makes his stomach wobble like a foundering ship; with a large shot of baking soda, which starts kicking around the carcass of the no-longer-Flippant Hen; and then with all the various and fearful cocktails composed of sauerkraut, pineapple, or any other kind of juice.

"If our Mr. Blop is a very strong man, he may hold out until noon before staggering to the nearest bar for something that will either kill or cure him.

"At the bar, other friends will flock about him and dose him with one of the following mixtures: (1) A suissette, composed of absinthe and white of an egg; (2) A sazarac, gaining its strength from rye and absinthe; (3) A Picon Bitters, made of Picon Bitters and lime juice, or (4) A Fernet Branca, a thick, black bitters with quinine in it.

"As a last resort, if our Mr. Blop is still suffering, some wise one may give him a Sea Captain's Special, so named because it was invented by a genius named Harry Porter in a bar on the Seattle waterfront to treat the hangovers of the tramp freighter captains who docked there for a spree, and who were notorious for the ferocity of their morning-after heads.

"The Sea Captain's Special is distilled dynamite. It is mixed as follows: In an Old Fashioned glass place half a lump of sugar and douse it with Angostura. Add one and a half jiggers of rye and one lump of ice. Fill the glass with champagne. Top it off with two dashes of true absinthe.

"As our Mr. Blop swallows this concoction, there is a sudden roar and the ceiling of the bar comes crashing down about his ears. He stands dazed for a moment, too stunned to move. Then, gathering courage, he dares to raise his eyes. There shining through the gaping hole in the roof, in all its splendor, is the sun!

"At this point we will leave Mr. Blop. He is feeling fine.

"As a matter of fact, he is drunk again. Tomorrow his hangover will be even worse.

"What is even more serious, he is courting alcoholism. If you do not believe the moralists who warn against the Hair of the Dog, then take the word of Mr. Richard R. Peabody, one of the world's greatest authorities on alcoholism, author of the book, *The Common Sense of Drinking* (Little, Brown & Co., Boston, 1939), who classifies alcoholism not as a habit but as a disease. Mr. Peabody says that the man who drinks in the morning to combat his hangover is courting the disease. Scientists, generally, support Mr. Peabody's contention. The Hair of the Dog is an assassin.

"Now let us consider just what happened to Mr. Blop so that finally he was forced to get drunk again to halt his suffering.

"It can be explained very simply: When Mr. Blop awakened, his stomach was paralyzed.

"The fallacy of all hangover remedies lies in this fact.

"Whatever is poured into a paralyzed stomach just lies there and, to use an inelegant term, rots.

"Cold water poured on a paralyzed stomach only makes the stomach more miserable. Black coffee will help a drunken man only if it is siphoned into him while he is still drinking.

"The stomach, while still paralyzed, cannot handle any kind of food or liquid. That fact should be easily recognized by anyone who stops for any length of time in order to consider the physiological effects of alcohol.

"What, then, *should* one do to fight a hangover?

"Nothing!

"It sounds ridiculous at first blush. It is certainly the hardest course to follow. But when one stops to think, the logic appears at once.

"The basic truth to be recognized is this: When you awaken with a hangover your stomach is completely worn out, drugged and paralyzed.

"More than anything else, it needs rest!

"The correct procedure is to treat the anesthetized organ as gently as possible and give it a chance to sleep it off.

"If our Mr. Blop had had sense enough to dose himself thoroughly with soda or any of the commercial alkalizing salts before going to bed, while his stomach was still awake and functioning, he might have felt better in the morning.

"These alkalizing medicines taken while the stomach is still twitching under alcoholic irritants, manage to do some good. Unfortunately, though, when Mr. Blop came home, he couldn't even spell 'soda,' much less remember to take it.

"To combat his hangover, Mr. Blop should have used some of the self-control which he forgot to use last night. And so must the rest of us.

"When the throat cries out for ice water, we must firmly shake our heads. If you were resting peacefully after a long hard night, how would *you* like to have someone come along and throw a pail of ice water on you? Your stomach feels the same way.

"If the mouth is so dry that it is unbearable, then simply wash it out with water.

"Upon arising, try to force yourself to do a little mild exercising. If exercise seems impossible, go to the open window and breathe deeply as many times as you can stand it. An oxygen tent is the one real aid to a hangover, but so few homes are equipped with oxygen tents nowadays that deep breathing must be accepted as a substitute.

"Don't take a bath unless you feel you absolutely must.

"If you *must* sit at the breakfast table, then call for half a cup of warm water and sip it slowly. The warmth may help your stomach. At least it won't hurt it.

"Clench your teeth and go to the office. Use a quick right hook on the first person who suggests a nostrum. It will discourage others. The exercise will be good for you, too.

"Use all your will power and concentrate on your work. Or at least go through the motions.

"Don't look at the water cooler.

"By ten o'clock or ten-thirty the cold whale fat in your stomach will begin to stir. By eleven o'clock you may feel actually hungry. If so, the worst is over. Your stomach has slept it off. You are going to live!

"You may now safely take an alkalizing salt or a laxative. Your stomach is ready to handle it.

"Earlier, it was stated that the Prairie Oyster and the tomato juice cocktail had just enough truth in them to make them plausible. At this point, the element of truth emerges.

"When the stomach begins to show signs of awakening and demands food, feed it something like a Prairie Oyster—or even one of those awful Flippant Hens! The Prairie Oyster, as you know, consists of a teaspoon of Worcestershire Sauce, a tiny drop of tobasco, a raw egg, and a sprinkling of salt and of pepper.

"The theory is this: Your stomach is still half asleep; so you send it down something to give it a kick in the pants, and then hand it down something easily digestible to eat. The tobasco and other condiments provide the kick in the pants. There is nothing more easily digestible than a raw egg.

"All hangover remedies, aside from the alkalizers, are based on this theory. Your tomato juice doused with Worcestershire, salt and pepper; your various other highly-seasoned or spicy mixtures—all of them are designed to give the stomach a kick in the pants and start the gastric juices flowing.

"But all of them fail if foisted upon the stomach while it is still incapable of reacting.

"The strange alcoholic mixtures intended as pick-me-ups are likewise based on the same idea.

"Most of them contain absinthe, because there is no more powerful stomach irritant than the infusion of wormwood root in that New Orleans delight. The others use some type of bitters as a substitute. The bitters are nothing but a stomach irritant: In ordinary drinking, they step up the absorption of alcohol; in case of a hangover, they provide the swift kick.

"If you will stick to your Prairie Oyster at about eleven o'clock, however, you will find yourself quite hungry at lunch time. *Eat lightly!* Eat something spicy or something covered with mustard—but don't eat much of it.

"Your stomach is still too tired to take on much work at this time.

"By mid-afternoon, you should begin to feel almost normal.

"By dinner time, you should be ready, with a fairly healthy stomach, for another round of drinks.

"And remember: If you can shake your head sideways until six o'clock in the evening, you're safe . . . Until the next morning, anyway."

And may we add—after our blithe opening to this chapter—a few sober reflections?

1. *Alcohol isn't Mama.* In his infancy, the drinks were on her and they were wonderful—warm, satisfying and soothing—turning his wails into coos and making him feel comfortably sleepy. As a well-known doctor expresses it, maternal milk is man's first anesthetic. But comes a time when diet broadens out in the direction of solids such as beefsteak and baked Idaho and milord is supposed to be on solid ground permanently except for soups and something to drink now and then. Even so, the subconscious mind carries memories of the simple life *chez* Mama which appeal nostalgically when cares and complexities get a man down in middle life. He yearns for consoling warmth

that will soften up his troubles and make him feel good. Alcohol will do this comforting job, but it can't solve life for him "like Mama did." It will take the cares off his back for an hour or an evening, but it can't carry them by the day, week or month. Certainly it will never lick them for him. And if he is so infantile, so unweaned as to imagine it will, he is a psychic sissy.

2. *Alcohol isn't business success.* It can be helpful in the form of diplomatic refreshments which build acquaintance and thaw commercial ice. But that's all, brother.

3. *Alcohol isn't a substitute for human society.* The ingrown guy who drinks solitarily because "the bottle understands him better than people do" isn't helping his troubles any. He is only thickening his shell. Doing so, poor hermit, with something convivial which, if normally used instead of misapplied for self-pity purposes, might have eased his shyness and gained him some friends.

4. *Alcohol isn't a solver of emotional problems.* If your gal has turned you down for the other fellow, or your marriage has hit the rocks, don't expect liquor to compensate. The label on the bottle makes no such promise.

5. *Alcohol isn't a cure for boredom.* The futile Mr. Yawn, who seems to have nothing on his mind but his ennui, somehow manages to think of a drink in the hope that it may make existence interesting for him, even momentarily. It doesn't.

6. *Alcohol isn't a protector against chill winds.* That feeling of warmth that you get from a shot of whiskey, brandy, or rum is caused by the liquor's trick of dilating the blood vessels and thus spreading a glow to outlying parts of the body. Perspiration portholes in the skin act as though aspirin were on the job. Hence the great outdoors is to be avoided unless the sallier-forth is well woolened up. But *after* exposure—ah, how welcome a shot of fragrant deshiverer! Old Man Winter can go jump in the river when there's hearthside steam of hot toddy or hot buttered rum, and then the hay.

7. *Alcohol isn't a stimulant.* On the contrary, it's a sedative, a relaxer. Upper story gets the biggest and quickest share, thereby shushing the Department of Don'ts and Restraints. Overdoses can unleash a whole pack of sleeping dogs, ranging from the frisky to the ornery. Moderate doses can set the conversational ball rolling and coax introverts to come out from behind their false whiskers.

8. *Alcohol isn't a diet.* It is a food, however, of a very special

kind, an ounce of 100 proof whiskey contributing about 100 calories, which the body uses as fuel. In an emergency, this prompt acting boost of energy is invaluable. But alcohol can't repair body tissues; only protein does that. And it can't chip in to the fuel reserve as do carbohydrates and fats, being strictly a short-time proposition. Appetite is sharpened by moderate amounts of alcohol. Immoderate amounts dull it and cause undernourishment by taking the place of the staples of sustenance which carry the vitamins that man needs. Wines, fortunately, do have vitamins, and so have the citrus juices of mixology. Beer's cereal cargo (carbohydrates) also contains some of these health items.

9. *Alcohol isn't a career.* Not even a part-time job. It's a recreation. Tension relief.

10. *And one last point: Alcohol doesn't mix with gasoline.* We are not sissies, and we too have driven apparently better after having a few than before. Yes, you are more relaxed, perhaps in a better mood to make those positive decisions and direct movements that sometimes avoid an accident. But some State authorities are physiological rather than psychological in their attitude. They say if you have had a couple of drinks, you'd better not drive. And they add—at sixty miles an hour your car is doing eighty-eight feet per second. This is the wrong time—facing a crisis—to be a split second—or forty feet or so—slow on the brake.

In other words, when you drink, don't drive, and vice versa.

As for the rest, you know quite well how stupid and annoying and downright troublesome and even dangerous a drunk may seem to you when you're thoroughly sober. So when you're in your cups, try to tuck away in your mind somewhere that *you* are that undelectable drunken bum, and not the charming, daring, seductive, brilliant, lovable, heroic creature you seem to yourself.

A good rule, perhaps. Be merciful with other drunks. Don't hit them, you may hurt them and be sorry. Don't humor them, they may stay with you and you'll be sorry.

Better advice. Avoid them.

Best advice. Don't be one.

Said Cicero: "Let us drink for the replenishment of our strength, not for our sorrow."

Amen.

AND SO—

Experience has taught us that drinking of alcoholic beverages is one of the great boons of the human animal. A slide from grace, and you will swear never to touch another drop. It is not hard thus to swear, because you're positive you couldn't possibly touch another drop anyway. But there comes a softening of resolve with the sinking of the sun, a desire to relax with this gift from the gods. Then you will regret careless words, heedlessly spoken, and once more reach gently for stirrer and jigger, for ice and decanter.

Fear not, at this point, for many are with you. And if you—in your hopeful lifting up of the heart—need additional support, we tender it to you herewith. Here is you *raison d'être* for a party on every day of the year. May it lend agility to the step, forwardness to the hand, a chuckle to the voice, and bring a tune to your heart.

Read then, and rejoice.

And rejoicing, drink once more to your great and abiding good luck that you are alive in this questionable and terrible and wonderful and exasperating world, alive among your friends, and with a good cheer close to hand, a gift of the earth around you.

A toast then that you never lack a reason for the joy that comes of things of the Spirit.

365 EXCUSES FOR A PARTY

Here's your new line on parties and why to throw them. There's an excuse for every day of the year, and every one authentic.

JANUARY

1 Happy Hangover Day
2 Today the sun reaches its closest point to the earth
3 The Planet Mercury is visible
4 The Anniversary of the OPM working on rubber rationing
5 Anniversary of the National Red Cross
6 Swap Day
7 Birthday of Millard Fillmore
8 151st birthday of Lowell Mason
9 On this day Mickey Rooney applied for a marriage license
10 On this day Skeezix of the funnies landed a new job
11 Anniversary of the meeting of the Federation of Women's Clubs
12 Anniversary of Saks gigantic sale
13 Buy Defense Stamps Day
14 On this day the 1 a.m. curfew for bowlers was declared
15 Beer shortage in London in '42
16 Anniversary of the 18th Amendment
17 Birthday of Ben Franklin
18 Anniversary of the opening of the Scrap Salvage Office
19 Birthday of Robert E. Lee
20 Inauguration Day
21 On this day 15 years ago grapes were $6 a lb. in London
22 Anniversary of the Hail America Golf Tournament
23 Anniversary of the U. of Chicago two-year degrees
24 Anniversary of the discovery of gold in California

25 Anniversary of the WPB girdle regulations
26 Birthday of Jiffy the Giraffe
27 Anniversary of the tearing down of Honeymoon Bridge at Niagara Falls
28 Annual snowball fight of Rinkeydinks
29 Birthday of Wm. McKinley
30 Birthday of F.D.R.
31 On this day Ann Shirley sued for her divorce

FEBRUARY

1 First anniversary of the order prohibiting juke boxes
2 Groundhog Day
3 Birthday of Sidney Lanier
4 Anniversary of meeting of American Social Hygiene Assn.
5 Constitution Day in Mexico
6 Birthday of Babe Ruth
7 Birthday of Charles Dickens
8 Anniversary of the N. Y. Dog Show
9 Feast Day
10 Anniversary of the unification of Upper and Lower Canada
11 Edison Day
12 Lincoln's Birthday
13 Birthday of Grant Wood
14 Valentine's Day
15 Susan B. Anthony Day
16 Mule Day
17 Anniversary of the P.T.A.
18 Eve of the Marine invasion of Iwo Jima (1945)
19 Anniversary of the International Council for Exceptional Children
20 Birthday of Gloria Vanderbilt
21 Anniversary of dedication of Washington Monument
22 Washington's Birthday
23 Anniversary of the Red Army
24 Independence Day in Cuba
25 Anniversary of the launching of the *Kingsfish,* a submarine
26 Birthday of Victor Hugo
27 International Day
28 Anniversary of the Chinese Feast of the Lanterns

MARCH

1 State Day in Nebraska
2 Texas Independence Day
3 Anniversary of the Child Labor Law
4 Anniversary of meeting of U. S. Congress
5 Anniversary of bank holiday
6 Anniversary of the meeting of the American Chemical Society
7 Masaryk Day for Czechs
8 Farmer's Day
9 Anniversary of the battle between *Monitor* and *Merrimac*

10 Anniversary of Albany as the capital of New York
11 Anniversary of the Lease-Lend Act
12 Anniversary of the Girl Scouts
13 Anniversary of the discovery of the planet Pluto
14 Birthday of Albert Einstein
15 Anniversary of the abdication of the Czar of Russia
16 Birthday of James Madison
17 St. Patrick's Day
18 Birthday of Grover Cleveland
19 Anniversary of the National Defense Mediation Board
20 Anniversary of "Uncle Tom's Cabin"
21 Anniversary of the St. Louis Dog Show
22 Emancipation Day in Puerto Rico
23 Birthday of Larry Chittenden
24 Anniversary of Library of Congress
25 Lady Day
26 Anniversary of the Milwaukee Public School Music Festival
27 Anniversary of the Greensboro, N. C., open golf championship
28 Anniversary of the end of the Civil War in Spain
29 Anniversary of Canada's Constitution
30 Seward's Day in Alaska
31 Transfer Day in the Virgin Islands

APRIL

1 Anniversary of the Cherry Blossom Festival in Washington
2 Anniversary of U. S. Mint
3 Anniversary of the Pony Express
4 Adoption of Act of Chapultepac, 1945
5 Bette Davis' and Spencer Tracy's birthdays
6 Old Lady Day
7 The birthday of Fala, F.D.R.'s dog
8 Anniversary of Ponce de Leon's Landing in Florida
9 Tommy Manville's birthday
10 Founder's Day in the Salvation Army
11 Anniversary of F.D.R.'s increase of national debt limit
12 Anniversary of the Passage of Halifax Independence Resolution
13 Birthday of Thomas Jefferson
14 Pan American Day
15 Anniversary of American T. & T. stockholders' meeting
16 DeDiego's birthday
17 252 days to Christmas
18 Anniversary of Paul Revere's ride
19 Patriot's Day

20 Hitler's birthday
21 Queen Elizabeth's birthday
22 Arbor Day
23 Birthday of James Buchanan
24 Anniversary of the Drake Relay Races
25 Anniversary of the reunion dinner of the Fossils
26 Wedding of King George and Queen Elizabeth
27 Birthday of Ulysses Grant
28 Birthday of James Monroe
29 Birthday of Hirohito
30 Anniversary of the opening of the N. Y. World's Fair

MAY

1 Labor Day in the Canal Zone
2 Anniversary of the American Booksellers Convention
3 Semi-Pro Baseball Day
4 R. I. Independence Day
5 Anniversary of Napoleon's exile
6 Anniversary of the purchase of Manhattan by Peter Minuit
7 Birthday of Robert Browning
8 Joan of Arc Day
9 Golf Week begins
10 Confederate Memorial Day
11 Birthday of Henry Morgenthau, Jr.
12 Birthday of Florence Nightingale
13 Birthday of Joe Louis
14 Ascension Day
15 Anniversary of the Jumping Frog Derby of Calaveras County
16 Raisin Week begins
17 Anniversary of the assembling of the Statue of Liberty
18 Anniversary of the Norwegian Constitution
19 Spanish Orphan Day
20 Declaration of Independence Anniversary in N. C.
21 Birthday of De Soto
22 Maritime Day
23 Anniversary of the opening of the New York Public Library
24 Anniversary of the hanging of Captain Kidd in London
25 Anniversary of the National Spelling Bee
26 Queen Mary's Birthday
27 Anniversary of the sinking of the German boat, *Bismarck*
28 Birthday of the Dionne Quintuplets
29 Anniversary of Roanoke College
30 Decoration Day
31 Anniversary of the Johnstown Flood

JUNE

1 Anniversary of the separation of Kentucky from Virginia

2 Anniversary of stockholders' meeting of Standard Oil
3 Birthday of Jefferson Davis
4 Feast Day
5 Anniversary of the Ozark "Smile Girl" contest
6 Constitution Day in Denmark
7 Anniversary of Congress' approval of penny postal cards
8 Anniversary of the meeting of the National Confectioners' Association
9 Birthday of Cole Porter
10 Anniversary of the Portland, Ore., Rose Festival
11 Kamehamena Day in Hawaii
12 King George's birthday
13 Anniversary of the landing in France of General Pershing
14 Flag Day
15 Anniversary of Benjamin Franklin's kite experiment
16 Convention of the International Brotherhood of Magicians
17 Bunker Hill Day
18 Birthday of James Montgomery Flagg
19 Birthday of the Duchess of Windsor
20 West Virginia Day
21 Birthday of Rockwell Kent
22 Bolivarian Day
23 Anniversary of the National Baptist Sunday School Congress
24 Midsummer Day
25 Birthday of Jesse Straus
26 Anniversary of the American Crow Hunters Association
27 Anniversary of Fair Labor Standards
28 Birthday of Rousseau
29 Peter and Paul Day
30 Anniversary of the Y.M.C.A.

JULY

1 Anniversary of F.D.R.'s address to the Dem. Convention
2 Anniversary of the first elevated railroad in New York City
3 Birthday of de Champlain
4 Independence Day
5 Anniversary of Optimist International
6 Birthday of John Paul Jones
7 Anniversary of Barnard College's first summer session
8 Anniversary of Jacob's Pillow Dance
9 Anniversary of the meeting of the Society of American Florists
10 Statehood Day in Wyoming
11 Birthday of John Quincy Adams

12 Birthday of Henry Thoreau
13 Gen. Nathan Bedford Forrest's birthday
14 Bastille Day
15 St. Swithin's Day
16 Birthday of Amundsen
17 Birthday of Manoz Rivera
18 Birthday of Jane Austen
19 Anniversary of the first Women's Rights Convention
20 Anniversary of the Nat'l Shuffleboard Championship
21 Anniversary of Belgian Independence
22 Birthday of Mendel
23 Chippewa Day
24 Mormon Pioneer Day
25 Occupation Day in Puerto Rico
26 Birthday of Baron Rothschild
27 Barbosa's birthday
28 Anniversary of the 14th Amendment
29 Mussolini's birthday
30 Dog Day
31 Joseph Lee Day

AUGUST

1 Colorado Day
2 John Kieran's birthday
3 New World Anniversary Day
4 Anniversary of the Coast Guard
5 Anniversary of Chautauqua Institution
6 Deadwood Day
7 Anniversary of the founding of the Order of the Purple Heart
8 Anniversary of Daylight Saving time in London
9 Anniversary day of the first locomotive drawn by steam
10 Birthday of Herbert Hoover
11 Crossing of Niagara Falls on a tightrope wire by Blondin
12 Indian Day
13 Occupation Day
14 Assumption Day
15 Napoleon's birthday
16 Battle of Bennington Day
17 Anniversary of Fulton's first steamboat trip
18 Birthday of Virginia Dare
19 Aviation Day
20 Birthday of Benjamin Harrison
21 Birthday of Princess Margaret Rose
22 Birthday of Claude Debussy
23 Anniversary of the execution of Sacco and Vanzetti
24 Anniversary of Parcel Post
25 Independence Day in Uruguay
26 The 19th Amendment
27 Kellogg Peace Pact
28 Anniversary of the Bureau of Engraving and Printing
29 Birthday of Maeterlinck

30 Birthday of Huey P. Long
31 Anniversary of World War II

SEPTEMBER

1 Beginning of the oyster season
2 Fiesta of San Esteban
3 Anniversary of the Roof-top Harvest Corn Husking Match
4 Anniversary of the world's first electric power station
5 Fiesta of Santa Fe
6 Birthday of Lafayette
7 Birthday of J. P. Morgan
8 Magellan arrived from the first trip around the world
9 Admission Day in California
10 Anniversary of the subway in N. Y. C.
11 Manhattan discovered
12 Defender's Day
13 Birthday of Pershing
14 Anniversary of the Gregorian Calendar
15 Birthday of William Howard Taft
16 Anniversary of the Cherokee Strip Contest
17 Anniversary of adoption of Declaration of Independence
18 Gandhi's birthday
19 San Jose Day in New Mexico
20 Regatta Day
21 Anniversary of the beginning of George Washington Bridge
22 Execution of Nathan Hale
23 Anniversary of the meeting of the Association of Legal Aid
24 Anniversary of annual horse show in Monterey, California
25 Anniversary of the Assembly of Telephone Pioneers
26 Birthday of the King of Denmark
27 Gold Star Mothers' Day
28 Anniversary of the discovery of California
29 Leif Ericsson Day
30 Anniversary of Munich Pact

OCTOBER

1 Anniversary of the announcement of Sally Rand's engagement
2 Wedding anniversary of Governor James of Pennsylvania
3 Today the planet Mars is only 38,130,000 miles from the earth
4 Birthday of Rutherford Hayes
5 Birthday of Chester Alan Arthur
6 Missouri Day
7 Anniversary of Northwestern University's Pajama Contest
8 American Tag Day

9 Anniversary of Arkansas' Tribute to a Mule Pageant
10 Anniversary of the opening of the U. S. Naval Academy
11 Anniversary of the first ascension of the Graf Zeppelin
12 Fraternal Day
13 Anniversary of the Town and Country Equestrians
14 Anniversary of the Lithuanian Relief Dinner
15 Anniversary of lecture season of the Women's Athletic Club
16 Mothers' Day at Brookfield Zoo
17 Anniversary of Walgreen's Super-Value Days
18 Alaska Day
19 Anniversary of Medinah Temple Oriental Pageant
20 Alpha Delta Pi Alumnae Meeting
21 Anniversary of Washington Monument
22 Anniversary of the Barbers' Association of America
23 Anniversary of the launching of the submarine *Trigger*
24 Anna Taylor plunges over Niagara Falls in a barrel
25 Anniversary of the opening of George Washington Bridge
26 Anniversary of the Homemakers Conference
27 First mink bottle opener appears
28 Anniversary of the unveiling of the Statue of Liberty
29 Anniversary of the Illinois Cornhusking Contest
30 Buy a Doughnut Day
31 Nevada Day

NOVEMBER

1 All Saints' Day
2 Memorial Day in Canal Zone
3 Secession from Colombia Day in the Canal Zone
4 Anniversary of the National Roller Derby
5 Anniversary of the election of Al Smith as Governor of N. Y.
6 Anniversary of the meeting of the International Kiwanis Club
7 Anniversary of the meet- of the Gold Star Mothers' Club
8 Anniversary of the election of Governor Lehman
9 Mt. Holyoke Alumni Day
10 Anniversary of independence from Spain in Canal Zone
11 Armistice Day
12 Anniversary of the completion of the New York Subway
13 Anniversary of the Smoke for the Yanks Drive

14 Anniversary of ASCAP
15 Anniversary of a Notre Dame-Northwestern game
16 Christening Day of King Leopold
17 Anniversary of the English Speaking Union
18 On this day in '40 a box of Churchill's cigars sold for $2,010
19 Discovery Day in Puerto Rico
20 Anniversary of the National Crocheting Contest
21 Anniversary of the Mexican Revolution
22 Birthday of Garner
23 Repudiation Day in Md.
24 Birthday of Zachary Taylor
25 Anniversary of the Wheaton Anti-War Rally
26 Anniversary of the meeting of the American Dental Association
27 Anniversary of the meeting of the Snowchasers Club
28 Anniversary of peace between U. S. and Tunis
29 Byrd reached the North Pole
30 Bonifacio Day

DECEMBER

1 Anniversary of the Chicago Stock Show
2 Anniversary of the Monroe Doctrine
3 Birthday of Illinois State
4 U. of Purdue Queen Contest
5 Birthday of Martin Van Buren
6 Anniversary of placing capstone on Washington Monument
7 Anniversary of the opening of U. S.-Africa airmail service
8 Anniversary of the American Farm Bureau Federation
9 Birthday of William Henry Harrison
10 Fewer than 14 shopping days until Christmas
11 Anniversary of the Bank Moratorium
12 Anniversary of the American Pioneers Bridge Tourney
13 Anniversary of the Annual Hoosier Dinner
14 4-H Club meeting
15 Holiday issue of Esquire is on the newsstands
16 The Railway Business Women's Annual Yule Party
17 Anniversary of the first flight of the Wright Brothers
18 Anniversary of the Indiana University Dames Ball
19 The Big Sisters of the Off the Street Club Yule Party
20 Anniversary of Mid-Year Graduation at the U. of Chicago

21 Pilgrims landed on Plymouth Rock
22 Only 3 shopping days until Christmas
23 Anniversary of W. Wilson Foundation
24 Tom and Jerry Night
25 Merry Christmas
26 Anniversary of the landing of two baby pandas from China
27 Anniversary of the Chicago Bowling Tournament
28 Holy Innocent's Day
29 Birthday of Andrew Johnson
30 Rizal Day
31 Anniversary of the National Football Coaches' Assn. luncheon.